Camel from Kyzylkum
A Memoir of My Life Journey

Lara Gelya

Copyright @ 2021 by Lara Gelya
All rights reserved.
No part of this book may be reproduced or transmitted in any form or by any means, electronic or mechanical, including photocopying, recording or by any information storage and retrieval system, without written permission from the author, except for the inclusion of brief quotations in review.

Life Journeys Books—Valencia Lakes, Florida
ISBN (pbk.): 978-1-7377878-0-8
ISBN (ebk.): 978-1-7377878-2-2
Library of Congress Control Number: 2022906022
Title: *Camel from Kyzylkum*
Author: Lara Gelya
Digital distribution | 2022
Paperback | 2022

Published in the United States of America

Camel from Kyzylkum
A Memoir of My Life Journey

"There is no greater agony than bearing an untold story inside you."
—Maya Angelou

Table of Contents

Preface vii
Chapter One: The Desert 1
Chapter Two: The Beginning 5
Chapter Three: Geological Party #10 22
Chapter Four: Muruntau 28
Chapter Five: Zarafshan 34
Chapter Six: Yalta 50
Chapter Seven: Gomel 60
Chapter Eight: Exodus 62
Chapter Nine: Austria 66
Chapter Ten: Italy 75
Chapter Eleven: Buffalo 85
Chapter Twelve: Burger King 91
Chapter Thirteen: Calumet Arts Cafe 95
Chapter Fourteen: Greeley Street 99
Chapter Fifteen: Schools 106
Chapter Sixteen: Natasha's Arrival 110
Chapter Seventeen: My Friends 116
Chapter Eighteen: Dot-Com Bubble 120
Chapter Nineteen: Washington, D.C. 122
Chapter Twenty: Emmes 125
Chapter Twenty-One: Sparky 131
Chapter Twenty-Two: 9/11 145
Chapter Twenty-Three: Grandchildren 148
Chapter Twenty-Four: North Port 154
Chapter Twenty-Five: The Madness of the
Year 2013 163
Chapter Twenty-Six: The Precious Gifts of Life 175
Epilogue 184

Preface

Several years ago, my husband Sparky and I retired and moved to the west coast of Florida. Our 55+ active adults community is a little bubble of paradise with everyday sunshine, lush green landscape all around, and amenities that make us feel as though we're on vacation 24/7. We love the gators, birds, lizards, and wildlife. Being so close to the beach is fantastic! Never could I have imagined that my life's journey would bring me to such an incredible place, when over thirty years ago, on March 15, 1990, I landed in Buffalo, New York, with refugee status, alone, with no English and not a penny in my pocket. My life journey has been full of hope, adventures, hard work, constant learning, amazing friendships, disappointments, mistakes, dramatic turns, and happiness. There were seasons of Light, and seasons of Darkness. Bits and pieces of my life that raced through my mind transformed into words that have been etched on paper—they represent a significant investment of time, mental energy, and emotions.

I want to share my lessons learned, my tears shed, my battles lost, my battles won, and my journey to freedom from the Soviet Union. I want to share it all with the most important people in my life—my husband and our four grandchildren. I want to turn my life's journey into a gift of love and light for them. I do not want it to be lost or forgotten. I also want to provide all members of our combined families with a brief history of who I am and where I came from. Everyone has his/her own story. This is my story. It is not perfect, but that's okay. I hope it helps everyone who reads it to learn to never give up their dreams, to live life in wonderful ways, to love, and to hope.

A story told is a life lived.

Chapter One
The Desert

I was born in Ukraine and went to school there. But I spent twenty years of my life in the Kyzylkum Desert of Uzbekistan—from 1968 to 1988. I was working as a geophysicist at geological expeditions and geological sites for the exploration and excavation of uranium and gold.

The Kyzylkum Desert, Uzbekistan.

The Kyzylkum Desert is the fifteenth-largest desert in the world. It is located in Central Asia, in the interflow of the Amu Darya and Syr Darya rivers, a region historically known as Sogdiana. The desert is divided among Uzbekistan, Kazakhstan, and partly Turkmenistan. The name "Kyzylkum" can be translated from Turkic as "Red Sands." Turkic languages are a group of languages of the same origin, spoken in a vast area extending from Ponto-Caspian steppes, Balkans and West Asia to Central Asia. Kyzylkum is a sandy desert with ridges of dunes, many of which are covered with vegetation. Sands formed by weathering and fluttering of bedrock sandy deposits have a reddish color there. The desert surface has a gentle general slope from the southeast to the northwest, towards the coast of the Aral Sea. The desert has always been a place on Earth that people have experienced in awe. They say that the desert is a living creature that can either accept a wanderer who has invaded its territory, or not accept that person at all. It depends entirely on the nature and mood of both sides.

The Central Asian Gray Monitor Lizard, Kyzylkum Desert.

Camels are called ships of the desert. They walk calmly, swaying regularly from side to side. This is because amble camels always rearrange the hind and front legs of one side of the body at the same time, so their bodies sway like ships on waves. Camels are unique animals that are able to survive in harsh desert conditions thanks to their physiology. They are not afraid of heat, lack of moisture, and scarce food resources. Camels have three sets of eyelids and two rows of eyelashes to keep sand out of their eyes. The desert lacks natural enemies for camels, making it an ideal habitat for these animals.

Camel from Kyzylkum.

In my home, I have a lot of camels on display—they are made from wood, from glass, and from stone. They are symbols and dear memories of my "first" life, of my twenty long years in the Kyzylkum Desert of the Republic of Uzbekistan. I am a camel from Kyzylkum, too. Like a camel, I have adapted and found ways to help myself survive in the desert. As a camel stores his energy in its hump as part of its legendary ability to travel hundreds of miles without food and water, I stored the energy of my spirit to help me stay strong as I crossed continents alone, with two suitcases and $140 in my pocket in my search for a better life.

Chapter Two
The Beginning

For my grandchildren, K & C:
Your heritage: On your mother's side, you have 25% Jewish and 25% Ukrainian blood; on your father's side, you are 25% Irish and 25% Scottish. Your father was born in the United States, but his parents, Denis and Nancy, immigrated to this country when they were young. I know very little about their story and hope that someday they will tell you all about it.

***

In all of my daughter's official papers, her birthplace is listed as Russia. However, we never lived in Russia. We lived in a country that does not exist anymore: the Soviet Union.

I was born on May 12, 1950, in Vinnitsa, Ukraine, to a Jewish family. My mother, Julia, was a pediatrician, and my father, David, provided custom-tailored clothing (outerwear) made specifically for his clients. He made all of my outerwear from scratch, starting from my teenage years.

Vinnitsa, Ukraine.

My father was twelve years older than my mother. He was a soldier during World War II. Before the war started, my father had a wife and a child, but they were killed during the war. Soon after he returned from the war, he met my mother, and they married. When I was twelve, though, my parents divorced. The divorce seems to have punched a hole inside of me that it took forever to overgrow. Both of my parents began their own, different lives. My mother had my sister, Alla, with a man who died soon after Alla was born. My father married a woman with two sons. In 1991, my father, his wife, and her two sons—who already had their own families—emigrated to Israel. I visited my father in Israel in 1995, three years before he passed away. My mother passed away in 2004 in Gomel, Belarus, where she lived with my sister, Alla.

My father, I and my mother, Vinnitsa, Ukraine, 1951.

It was not easy to live in the Soviet Union when born to a Jewish family. I suffered discrimination for being Jewish during my entire life there. Being Jewish in the Soviet Union was thought of as a nationality and not a religion. In fact, in my time, we lived with a slogan: "Religion is poison for the people." Our family, like most around us, did not practice any religion —organized religion in the Soviet Union was highly suppressed and atheism was vigorously promoted in the years of my childhood. Most churches and synagogues were converted into warehouses or simply closed. So, I grew up no different from all other children around me—I played the same games, went to the same school—but from my earlier childhood, I knew there was some stigma that made me different from others. It was called the "fifth column" in the Soviet Union—the column, or line, in one's passport that lists one's nationality. When this "fifth column" had it written that one was a

Jew, somehow it made that person a less valuable human being. I remember how from earlier childhood I tried to grasp this concept, and I could not. I only knew that I was different, but I did not understand why.

When we lived in Vinnitsa, Ukraine, we had a wooden fence around our house; it was always marked with graffiti. Words such as: "Jews live here" were written, but "Jews" was the derogative word "*жиды,*" and I do not know if I can translate it into English. Children in mixed families—Jewish with Ukrainian or Russian parents—could choose their nationality from either parent. Needless to say, they would rarely choose "Jewish" when given the option. It was then when I decided that I would never get married to a Jewish man—I did not want my children to suffer from the "fifth column" in their passports as I had.

I never looked like a typical Jewish person, so people could not detect right away that I was a Jew, unless, for some reason, I needed to show my passport. On top of that, I was never eager to announce that I was a Jew. Therefore, very often I was in a situation during which my coworkers and even friends made disparaging and belittling comments about Jewish people. That was a time when I wished I could "fall through the ground." When I went to work and lived in Uzbekistan, there were very few Jewish people in the places where I worked. Discrimination among Russian people was against the Uzbek people. Nevertheless, as soon as people discovered that I was a Jew, I was treated very differently. It was made clear that I was not one of them. It was invariably insulting and humiliating. Only when I arrived in the United States did I learn what it means to be Jewish.

***

Some things in life you'll never forget. There are moments in our core memory that we hang on to closely because we don't want to forget. The ones that make me smile are the best. There are also moments that stand still and are chiseled into my mind like frames, as if I'm watching a movie. For me, the emotions are as raw as they were many years ago. These memories are among my most valuable possessions. There are also moments in my memory that I want to forget. They are hidden so deeply, almost erased, and never be brought to the surface again.

In my very early childhood, I was a happy little girl with braided blonde hair and a little snub nose. In Vinnitsa, I attended daycare while my parents worked. In the summer, my parents sent me to stay with my grandmother in Belarus. My grandmother lived with my mother's twin sisters, Inna and Mila, in the city of Gomel, in a small house on the outskirts of the pine forest. Since my grandmother was unfailingly working (she was a medical doctor), my two aunts, Inna and Mila, took care of me. They were fourteen years older than me. We spent a lot of time in the forest; I took naps during the day in the hammock with beautiful pine trees rustling above my head.

With my aunts Mila (left) and Inna, Gomel, Belarus, 1953.

Inna and Mila always made sure that I got enough nutrition for my health and growth. When I refused to eat their porridge, one of them, usually Inna, dressed in an old sweatshirt, with a broom in her hand, pretending that she was Baba Yaga, a ferocious-looking old woman from the Russian children's books. While I was hypnotized and watched her performance in horror, Mila shoveled spoons with the porridge into my mouth. I think this theatrical show was an everyday occurrence until I was about four years old.

When I was five or six years old, I remember walking with my aunts to the store on a boiling summer day. I was tired. I stopped and said to them, "It's so hot that I would like to take my skin off and walk only with my bones." Astonished with my highly expressive thinking, they laughed. As the years passed by, my expression metamorphosed into a symbol of that time of our lives and was repeated at family gatherings countless times.

On warm, summer evenings, the youth from the little street at the edge of the pine forest gathered on the porch of my grandmother's house. They swapped stories, shared laughs, enjoyed each other's company, and sometimes subtly flirted. The energy and laughter emitted on this porch represented the time when life was still carefree, unexplored, and in front of these young men and women. As I was always with my aunts, I was able to stay with them on this porch and still remember their friends by name, even to this day. It was the best time ever.

When I was six or seven years old, my aunts sent me to the summer day camp that was set in a sunny meadow of a pine forest—there were two dozen tents with beds, where we could take a nap during the day, along with one large canopy that served us as a dining room. All games and activities were held in the open air, right in the meadow. The gentle sun shone with warmth through the pine branches. The balmy, thick scent of resin filled the air, and the needles crunched softly underfoot. In front, behind, and on the sides, reddish pines stood everywhere, and only here and there at their roots did some kind of pale greenness break through the layer of needles. I loved to spend days in the camp with wonderful smells and scenes of the forest. But after a few days, my head began to itch. I had long, thick, light-colored hair, which I braided in two pigtails every morning. As my head continued to itch painfully, I washed my hair every day after camp. This went on for an entire month; for whatever reason, the adults did not pay any attention to my scratching.

When my mother came to take me back to Ukraine, she finally checked my hair. It was a lice infestation. My beautiful hair was immediately shaved. When I started school back in Ukraine, the children laughed at me, teased me, and gave me offensive nicknames. That year at school was very traumatic for me. The regrown new hair was much darker, but just as thick. Since then, I have not had long hair. It was always, and still is, just a short haircut.

Memories of the time spent with my aunts in early childhood always bring me a smile, while memories of them in later years are sad.

Summer in Gomel, Belarus, 1955.

I'm 5 years old, 1955, Vinnitsa, Ukraine.

When I started school in Vinnitsa, I learned how to play Russian checkers. Russian checkers (also known as draughts or Russian shashki) were played in Russia and some parts of the former USSR, as well as parts of Eastern Europe and Israel. It is very similar to international checkers, but some rules are different.

I became such a skilled player that I played simultaneously against several opponents, winning games most of the time. My love for Russian checkers has stayed with me all my life. I have even tried to teach my grandchildren to play.

***

During the time of the Cold War between East and West, the Soviet Union was closed off to outsiders. When the country entered a period of political "thaw," and the flow of tourists to the USSR resumed after the war, they were offered tours of Moscow and Leningrad. Other major attractions included Crimea and Volga cruises. A small provincial city like Vinnitsa was not to be included in this tour list. What made Vinnitsa special and open to foreign tourists was one of Adolf Hitler's secret bunkers, from which he and his generals monitored the Eastern Front during World War II. The bunker was built in 1941 and hidden in the pine forest. It was called the Wehrwolf, in reference to "wolf," the translation of "Adolf," Hitler's first name. The bunker was built by Soviet prisoners of war, most of whom were shot dead and buried in a mass grave after construction was finished. There is an elaborate gilded monument to be found in the nearby village of Stryzhavka for the estimated 14,000 victims who were brutally shot.

In 1960, when I was 10 years old, I met Nicoletta Champitte, an Italian girl about my age who traveled to Ukraine with her mother and father as tourists. This family immediately became a sensation in our little Ukrainian city. When the three of them walked on the main street of our sleepy little town, they stood out in marked contrast to all the natives of our city. A crowd of onlookers would follow them in great amusement. I was part of this crowd. I remember how beautifully they dressed. The good-looking father wore a classic, well-fitting, black suit; he had dark hair and brown eyes. The mother was a very attractive young woman, wearing an elegant, light navy, corduroy coat and stunning high-heel shoes; her dark, long hair was expertly pulled at the back of her head, her skin was ivory, her bright red lips grabbed anyone's attention, and her bluish-green eyes shone like diamonds. Nicoletta was the same height as I, with blonde, curly hair pulled into a bun at the top of her head and big, bright blue eyes. What struck me especially was her black patent leather shoes and white stockings. This family walked calmly and freely down the main street of the city, set apart by dignified richness and grace. At one point, they turned around and gestured to invite me to step ahead and join them. From the entire crowd of people who were following them, they chose me—I could hardly believe it! Holding my breath and trying to shake off my nerves, I walked with them for a while; we communicated mostly through body language—I did not speak Italian and they did not speak Russian. Still, though, we managed to learn a bit about each other and exchanged our addresses.

From that one amazing evening began years of communication between Nicoletta and me. She sent me postcards with a view of the city where she lived—Lecco on Lake Como in Northern Italy. There were white, gorgeous houses on the banks of the azure blue water of the lake, surrounded by lush, green mountains. These postcards were, to me, a window into a magical, faraway world. Once, Nicoletta sent me a little package with a beautiful silk scarf. I was skipping lunch at school and saving my money—I wanted to collect enough to send her a gift, too.

After several years, I moved out of Ukraine with my family; at that point, correspondence with Nicoletta ceased and communication stopped. But this story stayed forever in my memory and heart. I always hoped that maybe someday I would travel to Italy to find Nicoletta's magical city, Lecco on Lake Como, and the street where she lived—via Risorgimento 41. My hope materialized many years later. We traveled there in September 2016; we found the street and the house, but Nicoletta Champitte was no longer living there.

Lake Como in Italy, 2016.

Things were changing for the worse in our family as I grew older. My life changed dramatically when my parents divorced. We moved to Gomel to live in an apartment with three rooms. My mother and I, along with my retired grandmother, my Aunt Inna, her husband, and her little daughter Rimma, all lived in two rooms of the three-room apartment. An older woman named Rosa occupied the third little room of the apartment. A six-meter kitchen and bathroom were shared. Privacy was unknown to all of us. It was noisy in our apartment most of the time, and quite often very noisy because people did not get along with each other. When this was happening, I was going outside and walked on the street until things settled down; I hated this very noisy time. The apartment never felt like home to me. Around this time, my sister Alla was born, and I was sent to boarding school.

In 1956, speaking at the Twentieth Congress of the Communist Party of the Soviet Union, Nikita Khrushchev ordered the immediate establishment of a wide system of boarding schools for Soviet children in which "engineers of the soul" could hatch a new elite under ideal laboratory conditions. In reality, though, the opening of boarding schools in the USSR became an important social project aimed at supporting large and single-parent families that experienced serious financial difficulties. It was a social institution to save children from living on the streets.

The lack of connection with family and the inability to be alone at any point of time in the day, the inability to choose a circle of friends, the cruelty among children, as well as many other factors, all inevitably had a negative impact on the life of a child in a boarding school. I absolutely despised the school with all my heart and soul. Nevertheless, I did very well in classes; I had only excellent and good grades for all subjects. My two favorite teachers, who were in their early thirties, took me under their wings. One teacher was an unofficial photographer for the school and had a little room as his photo lab. He taught me photography and gave me the key to his lab. It was my sanctuary where I could escape from the strange world around me by reading a book or just spending some quiet time. The little room helped me get through the years when I was hungry for the love, warmth, and joy of family.

Boarding school in Gomel, Belarus, 1966.

After I graduated from school, I went to study at the Geological College in Kiev, the capital of Ukraine.

It was the summer I passed the entrance exam to the Geological College. I had no place to go before classes were to start in September, so I got a job as a cook on the small service ship that was navigating up and down the river Dnepr, delivering various services to big river vessels.

The Dnepr (Dnieper-Ukrainian) is one of the European rivers flowing in the territory of three countries at once—Russia, Ukraine, and Belarus. It starts in the Valdai Hills in the district of the Smolensk region and ends its long journey flowing into the Black Sea. Dnepr is the fourth-longest river in Europe, after the Volga, Danube, and Ural.

My responsibilities were to prepare food three times a day for the team of ten men who worked on our small ship. Approximately 40% of the crew was overwhelmingly young, while the rest were between 30 and 50 years of age. At that time, my cooking skills were less than subpar, but the man who was cooking for them before me did not mind teaching me. I loved the two months I spent on the little ship. In my free time, I lay on the deck and smiled, watching the passing green banks. Blue Dnepr, blue sky, burning sun, immense space of blooming, boundless, green steppe... The evenings at the end of the long and hot summer days were especially refreshing with a cool breeze from the river. Most of the crew were gathering on the deck. Some smoked, some told anecdotes, and some silently enjoyed the majestic peace of the passing day. At night, I slept in my little cabin. Everyone treated me very well, with courtesy. My cooking skills improved rather quickly. When the time came for me to start classes, the crew of ten men did not want me to go. They invited me to work for them the following summer. However, when one year passed and summer came again, a brand-new adventure was waiting for me.

After my first year in college, I went to my summer

internship in the mountains of Tajikistan. There I met Nikolai Gelya; he had just graduated from the same college as I was attending, and he got his first job in the geological expedition in Tajikistan. We fell in love. I was eighteen and Nikolai was twenty-two when we got married and went to work in the geological expedition in the Kyzylkum Desert.

With Nikolai Gelya, 1970.

Nikolai was born on December 8, 1946, in a small village, Grigorovka, in Ukraine. We never knew Nikolai's biological father. Valentin Gelya adopted him when he married Nina, Nikolai's mother. Nikolai resembled his mother, especially with his big, green-gray eyes, which he passed on to our daughter. Valentin and Nina had a daughter of their own, Lilya, who was around six or seven when Nikolai was about twenty-three.

Valentin Gelya lost both legs during a fire in the school where he taught. His recovery and fight for his life took more than a year. But he survived. Both of his legs were amputated just above the knee. Although severely handicapped, he kept a strong spirit and supported his family by fixing electronic appliances for his neighbors. He moved on a wooden platform with wheels, pushing himself off of the floor with custom-made, flat, wooden devices for his hands. He drove a specially-made for handicapped people compact car and was a good husband and father. I had a lot of respect for him, for his strong and kind character, and for how he was able to deal with his limitations with great dignity.

From corresponding with people in Ukraine, I know that in the late 1980s, first Nina, and then Valentin, passed away. Lilya was married twice and had children with both husbands: a daughter and then a son. She divorced both men and lived in Grigorovka, Ukraine. In the harsh years of the 1990s, I even sent money to her and her children, but then communication was lost, and I do not know anything about them at present.

Chapter Three
Geological Party #10

After we went to work in the Kyzylkum Desert, for the first three years our young family lived in the little settlement of the geological expedition with headquarters in Tashkent, the capital of Uzbekistan. Our settlement was simply called Geological Party #10. There were two dozen barracks houses under the blistering sun, in a barren area of the landscape that was lacking vegetation, offering hostile living conditions for human, plant, and animal life.

Geological party #10, Kyzylkum Desert, Uzbekistan, 1969.

We worked and lived literally in the middle of

nowhere. The closest civilized city, Navoi, was 200 kilometers (124.3 miles) away. The winter of 1968-1969 was unusually severe, even for a wild desert climate. Our little habitation got cut off from the entire world because of the severe weather. At night, under a wide canvas of the open sky, the wind flitted along the vast expanses of desert, picking up speed and ferocity, growing into a growling, tumbling sand and snowstorm. I could not fall asleep for a long time, as I was listening to the howling sounds outside. It was one of those winds that made the nerves jump, curl hair, and make skin itch. Our little aircraft stopped delivering products and food to us. Water and goodies did not come for days, sometimes weeks, as the passage in the sands was covered by snow and ice. We ate canned meat with macaroni and old, dried pepperoni sausages from our store's reserve. I stopped eating canned food and pepperoni after that winter.

We melted snow and filtered it from the sand to make water for our drinking needs. I dreamed about milk and apples. The fact that I was pregnant during that time made everything even harder. I think we survived only because we were so young and ignorant. Eventually, everything ends, and so did that unforgettable winter.

I could not see a doctor during my pregnancy because there were no doctors in our geological party. In fact, it was almost my due date before I saw a doctor for the first time. As my due date approached, we were ready to head to Navoi, where I was supposed to stay with our friend until my delivery date. It was the end of May. Sparse vegetation scorched by the desert sun had already turned brown and dry, the temperature was unbearably high during the day (around +50C/122F), and air conditioning was not available, at least not in the desert of the Soviet Union.

Navoi was founded in 1958. The city got its name in honor of the great Uzbek poet and statesman, Alisher Navoi. The city of Navoi is nearly a midpoint between Samarkand and Bukhara. In my years in Uzbekistan, it was never under the jurisdiction of Tashkent. It was administered and supplied directly from Moscow. The city was completely artificial; the grand boulevards, square parks, and rectangular apartment blocks represented the height of Soviet perfectionist ideology. The city of Navoi currently has an ethnically diverse population of 133,526. But in 1969, it was a 10-year-old city rising on the southern corner of the Kyzylkum Desert.

City of Navoi, Uzbekistan.

Nikolai brought me to Navoi, but he had to return

immediately to our geological party to continue to work while I waited for my delivery date. Right before he left, Nikolai went to a little radio station that kept in contact with our geological party by transmitting messages. He asked the radioman to send him a message as soon as the radioman received a phone call about my delivery. To make it easier for the radioman, he wrote a template of a message for him to transmit. It read something like this: "To Nikolai Gelya. Larisa has delivered a daughter/son and is waiting for you to come." The radioman promised everything would be okay on his end. Nikolai and I said goodbye to each other, and he went back to work.

Two endless weeks still lay ahead before our baby came. I didn't know anyone except our friend, so I started out anxious and lonely during those two weeks waiting for the baby. I was astonished to see Nikolai return just two days later. He, too, was wondering why I was still walking around with my big tummy. What happened was that the radioman got very drunk the day Nikolai left, and he saw the template of the message in front of him and transmitted it to our geological party for Nikolai: "Larisa has delivered a daughter (the radioman skipped 'son')." That's why Nikolai had to do an extra trip back to Navoi and then return again to his work before my delivery date. Excessive drinking was a common problem in the Soviet Union, and in the geological industry, it seemed especially pronounced.

Finally, on June 14, 1969, our daughter, Natalya Gelya (Natasha for short), was born—the radioman had been right about the baby's gender. The delivery went relatively easy (I spent only two hours in labor) and had no complications. Four days later, three of us were heading back to our little place in the middle of the desert that we called home. First, we took a train and then rode 60 more kilometers in the back of a big, heavy-duty truck, through the dusty passage in the sands, under the sweltering desert sun.

I was nineteen at the time and knew very little about how to take care of a newborn baby in such extremely harsh living conditions. We made milk from a dry powder mix—I still hate its taste even now. We cooked food on a make-believe stove: electrical spirals in the grooves of a brick. In the hot summertime, we slept with buckets of water near the bed—to make our sheets wet from time to time in an effort to cool ourselves. All of these adversities did not prevent us from being happy and enjoying our life together. We were young and had a lot of friends. Meanwhile, Natasha was growing. She started to walk and liked to play with camels that hung out near the cistern that held the water—we all used this water for drinking and cooking. Sometimes camels managed to open the faucet, then they drank as much water as they needed before walking away. We would get up in the morning to find out that we had no water until the next delivery was to be made.

One evening, while I was watching the sun go down where the dry brown land and always blue sky met, I thought, "I do not want to live here for the rest of my life. It is time to move out of here." Soon, in 1972, we had moved to a bit more civilized place—to the geological expedition in the Muruntau region.

With Natasha, November 1969.

Chapter Four
Muruntau

The Muruntau gold deposit in the Kyzylkum Desert in western Uzbekistan was—and still is—one of the largest individual gold deposits worldwide, with resources in excess of 5000 metric tons of gold. Discovered in 1958, it has been in operation since 1967 using an open-pit method. It is owned by Navoi Mining and Metallurgical Combinat (NMMC). Gold from the open-pit mine and underground mining was conducted via trucks and conveyors to the Besapan processing plant. In my time, the pure bricks of gold were sent by special airplane every day—directly to Moscow. First, a small village Muruntau was established near the field of the gold mining complex. Soon it expanded and transformed into a larger settlement.

Open-pit gold mine, Muruntau, Uzbekistan.

The Besapan processing plant, Muruntau, Uzbekistan.

Bricks of gold from the Besapan processing plant, Muruntau, Uzbekistan.

There was a daycare in the village of Muruntau that Natasha attended. I developed a friendship with Gutya Makarova; her daughter, Olga Makarova, became Natasha's best friend. Today, Olga lives with her daughter, Anna, in Moscow. Anna's father lives in New York City. At least twice a year they come to the States for a visit. They visited us once in Virginia in January 2011.

In Muruntau, Nikolai built our little sauna (banya) next to the house—it was a good reason for our friends to visit us. We did not have bathrooms inside of the house, and the house was more like a barracks meant for a temporary stay. On the weekends, Gutya, Olga, Natasha, and I liked to climb the Muruntau mountains that were just behind our houses. Sometimes, at night, we could see a big, red and orange, round object, UFO-like, rising slowly above the Muruntau mountains and slowly dissolving from the inside out. It was an unknown and mysterious sight that always caused excitement and fear at the same time. Perhaps, a new rocket or a new weapon was being tested at the Baikonur Cosmodrome or, perhaps, it was a real UFO. I preferred to think that it was a real UFO—I believe our planet Earth has been visited by beings from another world before, and, at that time, I wanted to imagine that, perhaps, they came again and I could see them descending down the mountains in their own inexplicable way.

Muruntau village, Uzbekistan, 1973.

We had a gray dog who had black spots; her name was Strelka. Strelka was not a purebred dog. She was just a pooch freely wandering around and sleeping under our porch. One day, we looked under the porch and discovered Strelka there with five cute little puppies. They were like their Mama—gray with black spots. Natasha adored little puppies.

One morning, when I took Natasha to daycare, as usual, I said goodbye near the gates. From there she always went into the building by herself, and I ran to work because I was almost late. When at the end of the working day I came to pick Natasha up from the daycare, I was surprised to hear from the teacher that Natasha was not there. What a stressful evening; we had searched for our daughter everywhere! After several hours, with no success, we collapsed on the porch absolutely exhausted and desperate. Suddenly we heard some strange noise coming from under the porch. We looked there and found our dog Strelka with not only her puppies but also our daughter—all of them were taking a good nap together. Natasha always had a way with animals, winning their love and trust. That is one story with a happy ending that I will never forget.

Our dog Strelka, Muruntau, Uzbekistan.

Our family in 1972, Muruntau, Uzbekistan.

First snow in November, our family in Muruntau, Uzbekistan, 1974.

Chapter Five
Zarafshan

When the airplane began its descent to the little airport of Zarafshan, the city appeared among ochre-colored dunes with clusters of standard blocks of flats built in the 1970s. They did not differ from the ones that could be seen in the outskirts of Moscow, Volgograd, or Novosibirsk. There were no monuments, tourist attractions, restaurants, or old buildings in the city. It was—and still remains—a mirage town, a ghost town, built by prisoners on Communist Party orders. The distance from Zarafshan to Muruntau is around 37 kilometers (23 miles) southeast, and "Zarafshan" translates from Uzbek to mean "gold-bearing". The sky was unusually clear almost year-round, and the sun was always bright. One could not hide from it. It was always there—above, ahead, to all sides, or behind.

Zarafshan, Uzbekistan.

In Zarafshan, we got a real apartment on the eighth floor of a nine-story building. It was 1975, and for the first time in our lives we were living in a real apartment building, not a barracks or tent, and we had a real bathroom and toilet, a kitchen, and two rooms with a balcony. There was no central air conditioning system for the building, and the window air conditioner was not known to us at that time. In the summer months, scorching, desiccating heat prevailed during the day, and nights remained hot long after the sun went down. These all made our existence tough, even in our new apartment. But it was a reality we could not change, so we adjusted our level of tolerance.

We bought our first set of proper furniture. Our nine-story building was in the center of the city, on Lenin Street. Across from our apartment building, the prisoners were building a movie theater, the only movie theater/club in the city when it was done. The prisoners were not in a hurry and would sit for a long time on the roofs of the buildings, observing life behind the barbed wire that surrounded the construction site. Very often they knew us, young women, by name and tried to initiate conversations when we passed by.

Our apartment building in Zarafshan, Uzbekistan.

From the eighth-floor view of our apartment, the horizon was open on three sides, and I could see far, far away. The biting desert wind was blowing through the city and falling stars streamed above the streetlights at night. The local weather center claimed that Zarafshan was the regional center of dryness. Sometimes, a very aggressive and strong wind called an Afghan ("Афга́нец") would blow over Zarafshan. The name was coined since it always came from Afghanistan. This wind could occur in any season. In Afghanistan, it is called Kara-Buran, which means "black storm," or body Shuravi, meaning "Soviet wind". When an Afghan began, it carried huge clouds of sand and dust. We could see it moving on the horizon. It resembled an enormous hurricane wave in the ocean, only it was brown. These clouds of sand and dust rolled through the city, through our apartments. Invisible to the eye, barely running in the air, thin, caustic dust penetrated everything in its way, leaving furniture in the house covered with a thin layer of sand, and it would get into all of the pores of one's skin. It had the distinct smell of sand. An Afghan passed through Zarafshan at least once a year, but sometimes more, and it became an unforgettable experience for me.

There were three special cities in the Kyzylkum Desert—Navoi, Zarafshan, and Uchkuduk. These three cities reported directly to Moscow and not to Tashkent, the capital. Also, they were supplied with goods and products directly from Moscow. Navoi was at the south end of the Kyzylkum Desert, Zarafshan was in the center of the desert, and Uchkuduk was north of Zarafshan. Salaries of everyone working in any of these cities were at least two times higher than average salaries in Uzbekistan or Russia at that time. Basically, we were paid more for the extreme living conditions in the Kyzylkum Desert.

Many evenings at sunset, I would stand on the balcony of our apartment on the eighth floor, gazing at the horizon where earth and sky met, and the sun was going down to disappear for the night, thinking about my life, trying to guess what lay ahead. For some mysterious reason, one evening, I thought, "Will I really live here in this desert all my life and never see America?" Looking back now, I have no idea why I thought about America at that time. I was not allowed to go abroad because of the place I worked and what was there—uranium deposits with mine excavation. But I guess some little piece of me knew or sensed that America was somehow my destiny.

I'm at work in a gold mine, Zarafshan, Uzbekistan.

Not long after we settled into our new apartment in Zarafshan, I discovered some big growths on the right side of my stomach. I went to see a doctor. Since doctors in Zarafshan could not figure out what was wrong with me, I ended up in the hospital in Navoi, where they were also unable to diagnose me. Therefore, they sent me to a special hospital in Moscow where I was diagnosed quickly. It turned out that I had a benign tumor engulfing my right kidney. I had the surgery and my right kidney was removed. I was twenty-five years old at that time. The girl who was in the same room with me in the hospital, and had similar surgery, did not survive. I wanted to be alive so much, and I was very stubborn in my determination! The first week after the surgery was terrible; I thought I was not going to make it. But then, little by little, I started to walk and do light exercises. I needed several months of rehabilitation in the rehab center in the suburb of Moscow before I returned to Zarafshan. Natasha stayed with Nikolai's parents in Ukraine through my ordeal. Finally, the family was reunited and back home after this twist of fate. I did not know that another turn of fate was just around the corner.

While I was trying to get back to my normal life and learn how to do it with one kidney and an open wound, Nikolai was working a lot—at least I was told so. He would leave for work early in the morning and come back home late at night. To my dismay, soon I found out that my husband was having an affair with my girlfriend from Muruntau, Olga Sirota. I learned it was even worse: Olga was pregnant by my husband. When people first told me this news, I refused to believe it. One evening I took a bus from Zarafshan to Muruntau and went straight to Olga's house. She opened the door when I knocked and I saw my husband there. My heart dropped to my stomach, and the walls in the room started to dance while my mouth became extremely dry. With cinematic clarity, I remember how they had a big pot with boiling water or soup on the stove, and my first impulse was to throw this pot at them; it took me a great deal of effort not to do this. My thoughts were very foggy. It was almost impossible for me to accept what I had just discovered: the unimaginable betrayal of our love and our life.

It was in the moment when I was the most vulnerable and needed so much moral and physical support. I got all of my strength together, turned toward the exit, and said to my husband, "Please pick up your stuff tomorrow morning." And I left. The next day I packed all of Nikolai's stuff and put it behind the door of our apartment. I was twenty-six and Natasha was about to start the first grade. There I was, alone, with a small child, in the middle of the desert, with an open hole on the right side of my body, and no one around me to talk to, cry to, or ask for help.

When some years had passed and the pain of the discovery of my husband's betrayal and the divorce subsided, Nikolai and I concluded that since we shared a child, we had to learn to coexist in peace. Sometimes, for a summer break, Natasha went to his house. He married Olga Sirota, the one with whom he'd had an affair while I had been fighting for my life. They moved from Muruntau to a different part of Uzbekistan and had two children: daughter Anna and a few years later, a son named Anton. They divorced in 1995. Olga took the children and moved to Vologda, a city with long winters in northwest Russia, well-known for its famous traditional lace handicraft. Nikolai moved to Uchkuduk, Uzbekistan. Many years later, Olga Sirota passed away in Vologda, on February 11, 2019, after battling cancer for three years.

From May to September, Natasha and I both suffered from severe allergies. I always tried to send Natasha out of Zarafshan for summer break to minimize her suffering—she would go to Nikolai's house or to Yalta, Crimea, where my Aunt Mila lived with her family. One summer, when Natasha was away from Zarafshan, I was remodeling our apartment. I covered our bathroom's walls and floor with tiles, painted the ceiling and walls, and replaced wallpaper. I did almost all of the work by myself, but occasionally, a friend helped me. One morning I looked in the mirror and was terrified—I did not have a face. Instead, there was a swollen mass with little cracks for my eyes. I ran to the emergency room for help. They diagnosed me with Quincke's disease (отек Квинке), angioneurotic edema (or angioedema), a form of localized swelling of the deeper layers of the skin and fatty tissues beneath the skin. I was treated in the emergency room and went back home the same evening. My condition gradually improved in the next few days. What exactly caused it was (and still is) unknown.

What else stayed in my memory is the day when Natasha had an appendicitis attack. We went with her to the movie theater across the street from our house, and she started to complain about pain on the right side of her stomach. When the movie was over, she was in such pain that I almost had to carry her to our eighth-floor apartment. I had to call for an ambulance soon after that. The surgery was done on the same night. It was a sleepless night for me. I was in the hospital nervously pacing back and forth near the surgery room, then sitting near her bed, frightened, worrying, trying to ease her pain. Later on, she endured weeks of recovery.

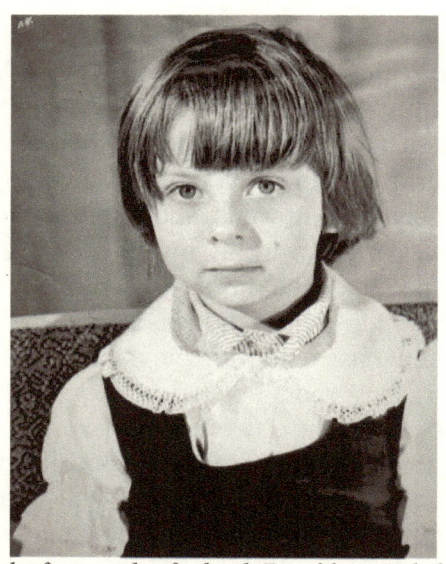
Natasha in the first grade of school, Zarafshan, Uzbekistan, 1976.

Natasha on vacation with me on lake Issyk Kul, Kyrgyzstan, 1980.

In the fall of 1983, students in Zarafshan were sent to harvest cotton in the fields of Uzbekistan. As I mentioned before, three cities in the Republic of Uzbekistan—Navoi, Zarafshan, and Uchkuduk—reported directly to Moscow and were not under the jurisdiction of Tashkent. For this reason, our school children had never before been sent to harvest cotton, even though it was a common practice with all other city schools of Uzbekistan. I do not know why it was different in the fall of 1983, but our local city government gave schools an order to send students from grades seven to ten to the cotton fields for two months instead of attending school.

A group of mothers revolted against this order. We sent a letter to Moscow with demands to stop the practice of using our children as slaves for labor on Soviet plantations. In response to our letter, a group of representatives soon arrived in Zarafshan from Moscow. They invited those mothers who signed the letter. They tried to tell us it was absolutely normal that our children be forcibly sent to pick up cotton instead of going to school; it was normal for these kids to work from sunrise to sunset for free; it was normal for them to live in poor and unhealthy conditions with the supervision of only one or two adults for over thirty teenagers. I remember how I asked the members of the commission from Moscow where their children were and why they did not send them to the cotton fields if it was so normal. I was furious and so were all of the other mothers. But we could not change the ways of our government.

Later on, I went to visit my daughter in the cotton fields. I worried about her. I do not remember the exact location, but it was many hours of driving from Zarafshan. Imagine four long huts standing parallel to each other, among the cotton fields in the hungry steppe of Uzbekistan. On the one side, there was a road beyond which there were cotton fields, and on the other side, there were just cotton fields. A small patch between the fields and the huts was the place of the "everyday life" of the students. Beds (Нары) in the barracks were made of slabs. The lower tier was for girls, while the upper one was for boys. The food they cooked was of poor quality. The labor was hard; after all, it was slave labor. There were cases when students committed suicide. I felt relief when my daughter, as well as other children, came back home safe, and life returned to its normal routine.

One of the most traumatic experiences we survived in Zarafshan happened on March 20, 1984, at about 2:00 a.m. Our few-month-old puppy, Dinka, started to cry at about 1:45 a.m. and woke us up. Animals can feel what's coming long before humans know about it. We tried to comfort Dinka, when suddenly we heard some strange noise coming from outside—it felt like the sound was coming deep from the Earth, and from the air, and from the roof of the building. Suddenly our apartment building moved back and forth in a wild rhythm, the furniture slid from the wall to the middle of the room, and things were falling. I looked in the kitchen and saw that our sink was dancing. All of this happened for about forty seconds, but it felt like forever. When I opened the door to the outside of our apartment, I saw people running down the staircase in underwear, screaming, "Earthquake! Earthquake!" We ran downstairs, too, and spent the rest of the night outside—we were afraid to go back to the eighth floor. In the morning we found out that the epicenter of the earthquake was close to the city of Gazli, about 245 km southwest of Zarafshan.

Natasha with our dog Dinka, Zarafshan, Uzbekistan, 1984.

Every day for the next month, or maybe even longer, there were a lot of aftershocks and tremors. I remember that many times at night I would have the same dream: I was in a boat in the open ocean. I would wake up and feel as though our nine-story building was moving again as a boat in the ocean—it was another aftershock. The original earthquake and its aftershocks made me feel like a little grain of sand lost in the endless universe—vulnerable, unprotected, unable to stop the danger. It was at the will of a merciful God or Mother Nature to save our lives or not.

A few weeks after the earthquake, we were informed that the foundation of our apartment building was damaged and all of us had to be evacuated. But evacuated to where? There was no spare nine-story building waiting for us. There were no empty apartments in the city where we all could move with our families and belongings. In fact, people had already been waiting for months and years to get an apartment. In Zarafshan, people could not buy an apartment at that time—all apartments belonged to the government and were given to those who worked in the mines or any other government-operated companies. No one was ready to deal with the aftermath of the disaster, so our local government decided to pack us into whatever rooms they had available. Our little family—Natasha and I—got a nine-meter room in a small, two-room apartment. We were supposed to share a kitchen, bathroom, and toilet with a family of three that got a bigger room in the same apartment. As if that was not enough, the connecting door between our rooms could not be locked and the man of the family had drinking problems—he was drunk, abusive, and dangerous every day after work. I was afraid to leave Natasha alone in our room, and I worried about her while I was at work. Plus, I did not know what to do with all of our furniture and other belongings that were still in our original apartment back at the damaged building. There was no way we could bring it all to the nine-meter room. I did not know what to do. Suddenly we had no place to call home. At night, I cried.

Very soon I realized that crying at night would change nothing. I needed to do something. So I went to talk with our city officials. I thought if I explained our situation, they might find a way to improve our living conditions. They listened to all of my complaints and remained absolutely indifferent. They told me they did not have an empty apartment available in the entire city where we could move and have a normal life again. I was in despair. My friends hinted to me that, in fact, there were empty apartments in the city that the government kept under lock just in case someone close to them needed it. I even got the address of one such apartment. It was away from the central Lenin Street, with blocks of charmless four-story buildings that had identical, boring facades. With the address, I went to the city officials again and asked them to give us that particular empty apartment because our current situation was unbearable and unsafe. Again, they said no.

Zarafshan, Uzbekistan.

I said to them, "You force me to occupy this apartment without legal permission because I have no other choices to save my child and myself." They could not arrest me for that because they knew that we were in an impossible position, and I had already asked them for help. But even if they could have arrested me, I had no other means to fight for our lives and our place to live. Some other families that had connections with people in charge improved their living conditions right away. I was a single mother with no connections to "important" people. All I could do was fight for our better life.

So I did just that. My co-workers and friends helped me to move our belongings from the nine-meter room and our furniture that was still in our apartment on the eighth floor, to an empty apartment on the first floor of one of the charmless buildings. I worked very hard to unpack all of our things quickly and make it look like we were living there. I knew that my battle for the apartment was not over yet. Leaving for work every day in the morning, I told Natasha, "When you are at home after school, do not open the door for anyone." But one day I came home from work just to find out that two strangers, husband and wife, were sitting on our sofa waiting for me. Natasha was crying—she had opened the door for them. They shook their legal papers right in my face—it stated that the apartment had been given to them officially. They shouted that we should vacate their apartment immediately. I promised them we would vacate the apartment the next day because it was late and we did not have any place to go. Cursing us, they left and said they would be back. It took many visits to the city officials, many curses from these strangers, and many tears and sleepless nights before we, finally, got an official paper for another apartment on the fourth floor of a nearby apartment building. By that time, I felt drained and exhausted, physically and emotionally, but I had won the battle for our home, for our life.

We had to move one more time. It was not easy to do in Zarafshan—there were no moving services available. I needed to ask for help from my male coworkers and pay them with bottles of vodka—that was the unwritten rule of the game. The fourth-floor apartment was the last place we called home in Zarafshan.

Natasha and I, Zarafshan, Uzbekistan, 1977.

Chapter Six
Yalta

Natasha graduated from high school in 1986. Nikolai and I attended her graduation ceremony. Soon after graduation, Natasha and I went to Yalta, Crimea, where Natasha planned to take an entrance exam for the medical school—she wanted to become a nurse.

Natasha and I, 1986.

1986 was also the year of the Chernobyl catastrophe.

The disaster happened on April 26, 1986. It was the largest accident in the history of nuclear power. The explosion occurred in the fourth reactor in the Chernobyl Nuclear Power Plant, near the city of Pripyat. Pripyat is located about 120 kilometers (62 miles) north of Kiev, the capital of Ukraine. That night, an experiment was carried out to measure the inertial rotation of a turbine generator. Overheating of the fuel caused the destruction of the reactor core. Another set of circumstances was also the cause of the nuclear catastrophe: first, the reactor had to be shut down before the experiment. However, it was decided to postpone its shutdown for later; second, less experienced specialists were involved during the night shift.

The Chernobyl disaster caused the largest uncontrolled radioactive release into the environment ever recorded for any civilian operation. Large quantities of radioactive substances were released into the air for about ten days, with the depositing of radioactive materials in many parts of the USSR and other countries in Europe. This accident caused serious social and economic disruption for large populations in Ukraine, Belarus, and Russia. Two radionuclides, the short-lived iodine-131 and the long-lived cesium-137, were particularly significant for the radiation dose they delivered to members of the public.

The Soviet government did not immediately inform the civilian population about this accident, and on May 1st, people in Kiev and other cities, without knowing about the danger, went to the May 1st demonstration, an annual holiday event in the Soviet

Union. Pripyat became a ghost city after the entire population of the city—around 50,000 people—were evacuated. All of these we know very well in the present day, but at the time we went to Yalta in the summer of 1986, the information was scarce and we did not yet understand the full scale of the Chernobyl disaster.

I remember that in the summer of 1986, there were an unusual amount of mosquitoes in Yalta and they were eating us alive. Never before or after, have I witnessed the same kind of invasion of mosquitoes in Yalta. Also, I remember that during that summer, one of the biggest Soviet cruise ships, Admiral Nakhimov, collided with a large bulk carrier in the perfectly tranquil Black Sea, and it sank. Around 450 passengers perished. It was absolutely devastating news at the time. I had seen Admiral Nakhimov many times in Yalta's port. I observed how women and men, dressed in clothes made of light fabrics, embarked on their journeys or disembarked the ship when their trips were complete. They smiled and seemed to be relaxed and happy—it always fascinated me as I was imagining their world, which seemed to have the makings of a glamorous, unknown life. I had never traveled on such a luxurious cruise ship, and I dreamed of being part of that world at least once during my lifetime.

From my childhood to the time when I left the Soviet Union, Yalta in Crimea was my favorite place on Earth. It faces the Black Sea on the southern shore of the Crimean Peninsula. For hours, I could sit by the sea and listen to the sound of the waves catching up with each other and breaking on the shore. I thought that by listening to the sea, I could learn to understand what it is talking about and what secrets it keeps in its depths. Yalta's scenic location between the sea and the mountains made the city one of the most popular holiday and health resorts of Ukraine, with many hotels and sanatoriums, including one established in 1900 at the behest of writer-physician Anton Chekhov. A sanatorium is an institution for the treatment and prevention of diseases by using mainly natural factors (climate, mineral waters, therapeutic mud, sea bathing, etc.). These natural factors are used in combination with exercises, a nutrition diet, and a certain regimen of treatment and rest. Sanatoriums were very popular vacation destinations in the USSR.

There were fruit-canning and tobacco-processing industries in the Yalta region, and wine was produced at the nearby Massandra winery. Yalta was a regular port of call for passenger ships from other Black Sea ports. The city was connected by roads to Simferopol and Sevastopol.

In Yalta, Crimea, 1967.

We could not stay in my Aunt Mila's house that summer because my cousin Rimma from Gomel, Belarus, came to deliver her first child in Yalta since the Chernobyl accident had affected Gomel. Elina was born in Yalta on July 4, 1986. Now Elina lives in northern Virginia and has two adorable boys: Benji and Mikey. In the summer of 1986, I rented a little covered porch for us in an old lady's apartment—just enough space to sleep at night. But for summer in Yalta, it was sufficient. After Natasha got accepted to medical school, I went back to Zarafshan—I still lived and worked there at that time.

***

Sparky and I visited Yalta in 2010 during our tour in Ukraine. We met all of our relatives there, including my Aunt Mila and her husband Josef, my cousin Serezha who worked as an ophthalmologist, and his family. My favorite uncle Alex, Serezha's father, unfortunately, had passed away by that time. He was a pathologist, but his wife, Aunt Inna, was still alive when we visited. My sister Alla and her children, Oksana (my favorite and only niece) and my nephew Sasha, arrived in Yalta to be with us as well. We had a great time during our visit. Every evening we walked the beautiful seafront promenade, watching happy people strolling by, busy restaurants, and street artists performing on every corner. Of all the cities we visited during our tour of Ukraine, Yalta stood out for the fact that people there seemed happy and free, enjoying life. Some special, unique spirit reigned there, and we felt almost good in Yalta.

Yalta, Crimea, 2010.

In March 2014, the Russian Federation annexed Crimea. The annexation from Ukraine followed a Russian military intervention in Crimea that took place in the aftermath of the 2014 Ukrainian Revolution. As a result, Yalta now is part of Russia. My Aunt Mila's husband, Josef, was brutally murdered in their own apartment in June 2015 while Mila was visiting her grandchildren in Moscow. It is still unknown to us who murdered him and why. Vitalik, Josef's son, already lived in the United States at that time, and my cousin Serezha from Yalta and his wife Lena were visiting us in Virginia.

***

Natasha's years in medical school were turbulent for me. In the first year, she was expelled from the school dormitory. I do not know what happened there with her. When I was able to come for a few days from Zarafshan to Yalta, she already shared a room in an apartment with other girls. But since that time I always had concerns—had a life away from home shaped her into a harsh person? What could I do from such a distance? I could not get more time away from work and felt helpless to influence my daughter's behavior. I wrote her letters, but I was afraid it was not enough. It made me upset and constantly worried about her. All I could do was to hope that she had enough common sense to stay on the right path in her life. There was nothing else I could change at that time.

Natasha in Yalta, 1987.

Meanwhile, the period of Perestroika and Glasnost started in the Soviet Union. Perestroika, (Russian for "restructuring") was a program characterized by the desire to reform society, to overcome the spiritual and moral crisis of the previous era of "stagnation". It was instituted in the Soviet Union by Mikhail Gorbachev, the general secretary of the Communist Party of the Soviet Union at the time.

Glasnost was understood as the movement in the USSR towards greater openness and dialogue. In the period from 1987-1991, Glasnost became synonymous with "publicity," "openness," and it reflected a commitment by the Gorbachev administration to allow Soviet citizens to publicly discuss the problems and potential solutions of their system.

I still lived in Zarafshan and took an active part in Perestroika and Glasnost—I was not afraid to express my opinions or attend meetings. I truly believed that we could change life for the better. One day I came to work only to find out that agents from the KGB had searched my office. KGB stands for Komitet Gosudarstvennoy Bezopasnosti, which translates to "Committee for State Security" in English.

At the time of Perestroika and Glasnost, books that previously had been available only through the underground distribution in the Soviet Union became legal, and excerpts were printed in many publications. I read a lot, and these books opened my eyes to the bloody recent history of our country—from the 1918 Revolution to the present day, on to all of the misleading, hidden truth, hypocrisies of our government, and the Soviet system as a whole. I realized that all of the concepts and ideas that they had taught us from early childhood were mendacious.

I learned about the Red Terror of 1918-1922—a policy of the Soviet state that legalized a complex of extremely cruel, repressive measures outside of the judicial system. The blows were inflicted on the disgruntled workers, peasants, and intelligentsia. In 1922, after the end of the Civil War, there was the last outbreak of the Red Terror, directed against the priests.

Then, from 1930-1950, innocent people were arrested on fabricated charges and tortured in order to force them to confess to crimes they did not commit. Thousands were shot or sent to the GULAG, where they died in the unbearable conditions of the labor camp. "GULAG" is an acronym for General Administration of Camps. It was a system of forced labor camps. Most camps of GULAG were located in the Kolyma, Magadan region of Siberia. The prisoners of GULAG built roads, houses, and bridges, and they mined gold, tin, and uranium. It was the prisoners who created the economy of the Magadan region. Those who survived remained to live in Kolyma after the release; they were not given the right to leave the territory. This terror was unleashed by Joseph Stalin.

There was displacement and deportation of national minorities, as well as mass deportations as part of the re-Sovietization of the Baltic States, Western Ukraine, and Moldavia. It was evidently impossible to give a full account of all of the victims of massacres, punitive treatments, and tortures.

These repressions were a major centralized operation against the civilian population of our country. Millions and millions of people perished. This discovery gave me a feeling of great sadness; it gave me a feeling of having been deceived.

These feelings and some other events in my life forced me to move out of Zarafshan. I did not have any more obligations to keep our apartment as a home for my daughter—Natasha was on her own path in life. It was time for me to make changes. My sister Alla came to help me pack some of my belongings and sell or give away the others. I moved to Gomel, Belarus just before New Year's Day, 1988.

Chapter Seven
Gomel

In Gomel, Belarus, I settled in a small room that belonged to my brother-in-law in a two-room apartment. The bigger room of this apartment belonged to a family of four—husband, wife, and two small children. We shared the kitchen and the bathroom.

I hated my life in Gomel. The city had many problems after the Chernobyl accident, and my salary was so low that I could barely provide for myself before the next paycheck. In Zarafshan, my salary had been doubled before I left. In Gomel, I was working in the photo lab at the Gomselmash, a manufacturer of agricultural machinery. My job responsibilities were to take pictures of production leaders and different events, so we could display them near the main entrance. I have liked photography since childhood, but this work of taking pictures of production leaders of the Gomselmash was just boring. I did not like the job, I did not like the city, I simply did not like to live there. Without the friends whom I had back in Zarafshan, I felt very lonely in Gomel. It also seemed that people in Gomel were quite different from people in Zarafshan. There was a very special spirit of camaraderie, friendship, mutual assistance, and solidarity among people in geological communities in the Kyzylkum Desert—qualities that I value immensely. It is because of what they had to go through together to survive in extreme living and working conditions. I saw none of these values in the people of Gomel; therefore, it was difficult for me to make friends there. I lived there only a little more than one year. Big changes were waiting for me around the corner.

Gomel, Belarus, Railroad station.

Chapter Eight
Exodus

The late 1980s were years of exodus from the Soviet Union. Gorbachev opened the door of the "iron curtain" and everyone who could escape was leaving. Every day, platforms at the Gomel railroad station were full of people: families who were lucky to get exit visas, and relatives and friends who came to say their last goodbyes to them.

From a book titled *The Svetlana Boym Reader*:

There was a code word: "to leave." If you whispered it with a mysterious gravitas, there would be no need to ask further questions. To leave meant to flee once and for good. You knew well your point of departure, but not necessarily your destination. To leave was an intransitive verb that marked a break in space and time. You might as well be going to the moon or to the Underworld. Farewell parties in the 1970s and 1980s resembled funerals in their finality.

When I was asked if I would consider leaving, I said "yes" with no hesitation. I did not know what leaving would entail, but I started to go through the process as everyone else did. I apprised the family members, but there was no need or time to have long discussions—

it was a once-in-a-lifetime chance, and the "iron curtain" could be down again at any time. We all knew how challenging and frightening immigration could be, but we had hope that after all of the suffering, we could build a better life.

I remember I was asked to provide a lot of original documents and go from one office to another. I spent a lot of time in Moscow and on the train from Gomel to Moscow and back again. The lines were enormously long, whether at the American Embassy in Moscow, banks for money exchange, or other numerous offices—to stay in line could take many hours or even days. Very often, the officials who asked me to provide another piece of reference paper—"spravka"—breathed vodka fumes on me. It took several months of traveling between Gomel and Moscow before I finally got my exit visa. I was stripped of my USSR citizenship as a punishment for leaving. All of my possessions were given away or sold—I was allowed to have with me only two suitcases and $140 at the time I exited the country. It was the point of no return. My goal was to reach America, but I was not sure if it would be possible, as the exit visa from the USSR was my only document. I promised my daughter that wherever I ended up, I would bring her there. We both knew that staying in the country we were born in did not bode well for the future.

The moment of my departure from the Soviet Union will be etched in my memory forever. I bought a train ticket to Vienna, Austria. By that time, the end of October 1989, I was totally drained, physically and emotionally, from my preparations to exit and by the uncertainty of the future. My father—he was 77-years-old at the time—and Natasha came to Brest, a city in Belarus at the border with Poland, to say their last goodbyes to me. I was walking on the platform to get to my train car, hauling my two suitcases behind. The iron fence separated the platform from the rest of the world. My daughter and my father hugged the iron rods from the other side of the fence and tried to scream their last words of goodbye. Their eyes were full of tears. None of us was certain that we ever would see each other again.

In 1991, when my father became brave enough to leave the country, the immigration process I went through was already closed; he, with his family, could go only to Israel. The same happened with my Aunt Inna and her son, Vova—even though they left soon after me, but they could go only to Israel, while her daughter, Rimma, was already in the United States. After a few years, Inna was able to reunite with her daughter Rimma via a family reunification program. Vova stayed in Israel until 2013. The Exodus from the Soviet Union tore many families apart.

The room where we were going through customs control was full of people—they, like I, were at the point of exiting the USSR for good, in hopes of finding a better life. Most of them were three generations of families: grandparents, parents, and children. I think I was the only solo traveler there. The two suitcases (for each person) that we were allowed to take with us were thoroughly searched by customs control officials. The rule was that if you did not give a bribe in advance, before you arrived at that point, you could miss your train. It was fine underground working order. My father gave 200 rubles to a special man—his job was carrying luggage at the station—and he was an initial point of contact in this well-functioning "enterprise." The man shared the bribes with those who were searching our suitcases. So, I was lucky that all of my belongings, carefully packed by me, were not taken out, and I was not late for my train.

It was a sleepless night on the train to Vienna. There was no place to sit—our suitcases occupied the shelves, and we made an open space for children and elderly people. The rest of us stood. Every time the train passed the border of another country, armed soldiers checked every car of the train, demanding our documents. All of these stops made me very anxious. When the train finally arrived in Vienna the next morning, I felt exhausted, yet happy, to reach my first destination.

Chapter Nine
Austria

I got off of the train and was not sure what to do next. Suddenly I saw a stumpy man with glasses speedily walking on the platform and shouting out: "Who is from the Soviet Union? Come with me!" The man was a representative of the HIAS, the Hebrew Immigrant Aid Society.

HIAS rescues people whose lives are in danger for being who they are; the organization protects the most vulnerable refugees, helping them build new lives and reuniting them with their families in safety and freedom. HIAS advocates for the protection of refugees and ensures that displaced people are treated with the dignity they deserve. It was established in 1881 to aid Jewish refugees from Eastern Europe. In 1975, the State Department asked HIAS to aid in resettling 3,600 Vietnamese refugees. Years later, in 2002, HIAS officially expanded its mission to help non-Jewish refugees.

From that moment on, starting in Vienna, my legal status in this world was as a refugee, and I was led by HIAS on my way to the United States of America.

When I stepped outside of the big railroad station in Vienna for the first time, I was shocked—in front of me I saw the dazzling, magnificent world with classy, shining cars coming and going, beautiful ladies in stylish fur coats and high heels getting out of cars, and tastefully dressed gentlemen helping them out. Station Square was busy but spotlessly clean. Tired, in my Soviet-style coat and knitted-by-myself hat, with my having-seen-better-days boots, dragging two heavy suitcases behind me, I felt like Cinderella at the ball of unknown life. It was unreal, like a shot in a movie. Today, thirty years later, I still remember this feeling like it happened just yesterday.

All of us who arrived from the Soviet Union gathered in one place and then climbed aboard the buses waiting near the railroad station. There were three buses, and they all took off in different directions.

Unfortunately, I saved no names of the places in Austria in my memory and I have no paper or picture trails left about my travels there. However, what is saved in my memory are my emotions and my reactions to everything I discovered while there.

Our bus brought our group of people to a gorgeous place high in the Alps mountains. There were about four houses in the tiny village, as well as a hotel and an RV park. It was a place where people were coming for skiing or for hiking in the mountains. Some of us were put in the hotel and others were assigned to the private houses—I was among the latter group.

The house I was placed in was quite big, with simple but comfortable furniture and decor, and it was exceptionally clean. The owners, husband and wife, were in their late sixties and retired. They were very kind people, and the husband liked to make jokes—we knew that because he tried to explain his jokes to us. They spoke only German and we spoke only Russian, so our communication was by gestures and guesses. I and another woman who was traveling solo—Lilya—were placed in the same room and shared one king-size bed. What has stayed in my memory from that home was a down blanket/comforter—it was so cozy and warm to sleep under this blanket on cold winter nights, and it was fluffy and weightless as a cloud. We shared the bathroom with another family that had a room on the second level of the house, next to us. On the first level, I think, two more families had rooms. The food was provided for us in the restaurant at the hotel, and we did not have to pay for it—it was paid for by HIAS. A special time for breakfast and dinner was allocated in this restaurant just for the refugee group.

Our group was comprised of Jewish and Russian families or mixed families, and three solo traveling women, including me. Some images are imprinted in my memory from that time. For instance, one young family that stood out included a husband and wife with five children, from six months to five or six years. The wife was an absolutely beautiful woman with dark, free-falling hair that reached her waistline. Her manners were calm and splendid, her posture displayed pride and competence, and positive energy radiated from her. The husband was very cordial, and the children well-behaved, but the wife was definitely the moral and spiritual center of this religious family—they all said grace before a meal, not something I saw often in the Soviet Union. I wondered how they could manage to be so calm and collected with five little children in a situation where they had to leave everything behind and did not know what lay ahead.

Another image in my memory is of a Russian peasant woman in her sixties, from a little Siberian village, dressed as a real Russian "babushka," meaning an old woman or grandmother. She traveled alone and had no family left in Siberia, nor any family waiting for her in the States.

The woman with whom I shared the room, Lilya, was approximately the same age as I was. She was a Jewish girl from Belarus, and she had never been married. Her parents stayed in Belarus and sent her to find happiness in a faraway land. A few years after we arrived in America, she got married and had a child.

I got friendly with a woman named Irma who traveled with her family. Her husband was named Leo and her teenage son was Daniel. Irma was a scientist from Minsk, the capital of Belarus. She was very attractive, intelligent, and bright. She was half Jewish, half Russian, and her husband Leo was also Jewish. Irma was already fluent in English. We liked to walk together and talk. Irma tried to teach me the very basics of English. They had relatives in Chicago where they finally arrived, and they chose to build their life there. Both of them did very well and got high-paying jobs. They also bought a house. Their son Daniel went to college.

Another memory from my life in Austria that will stay with me forever has to do with my first discoveries made in the closest little town that was five kilometers away from our village.

The road wound its way in the mountains covered with forest, dressed with the freshly fallen snow sparkling in the sun. Not far away, below the steep bank, the river roared along. The air was fresh and crisp. This five-kilometer walk among the sounds and scenes of the magnificent views of the Alps was therapeutic healing for my worn-out body and soul. One could walk all five kilometers without meeting any car or person on the road. I liked to walk this road alone. Sometimes, though, I walked with Irma.

As in any little Austrian town, there was a central square with a church, a government building, and a little grocery store. It was November when I visited this grocery store for the first time. I stepped inside and was amazed and saddened at the same time. The abundance of fresh fruits and vegetables that were neatly packed and on display was overwhelming, and there were so many other items I had never seen before. I was especially struck by the strawberries. They were bright red, ripened to perfection, packed in little wooden baskets, making them the center of attention. I could not believe that such strawberries could be in the store in November.

In the Soviet Union, even when in season, strawberries sold in the store were not so perfect and inviting. And other items in that store—why did I not know anything about them? It was a moment for me when I suddenly realized how miserable and undignified our life was in the Soviet Union. When I was a teenager, I spent long hours in line just to buy bread. When I was working, I stayed in line to buy some fruits and vegetables. It was a time when meat, sugar, flour, and so many other basic food products were rationed or not available at all. Yet, in the little store in Austria, everything was available and presented so attractively. There was something very dignifying about it. A sea of emotions swept over me and tears suddenly covered my eyes. I left the store and stood in the middle of the town's square, sobbing uncontrollably.

I had a lot to weep over: the life I'd led in my country of birth, not knowing that life could be so much better, that strangers could be kind and smile, that a visit to the store could be a pleasant experience. I wept about everything that I had to go through in order to leave my country. I wept about my unknown future. I wept until I had run my eyes dry of tears. It washed away all the sorrows of my soul; I knew it was going to be a tough and long road ahead, but I was ready for it.

One morning I woke up and discovered that my entire body was covered with a rash. I did not feel well. I questioned if it was an allergic reaction, or something else. I did not know. I was subsequently isolated in a little room on the first level of the house because our sweet hosts were worried that I could spread the infection to others. Few people know what it means to get sick in a foreign country without insurance and without money, although everyone can imagine. Fortunately, after several days, my body cleared up and I was back to normal again. But if it had turned out to be something more serious, what would I have done? How would it have affected the next steps of my immigration process? Would I have been left behind? I did not have answers to these questions and was happy that my condition cleared on its own.

At least twice our refugee group was driven to Vienna for interviews. I think it was at the American

Embassy or maybe some other organization that was helping refugees. All I can recall is that it involved a lot of paperwork that we needed to fill out, and a long wait to be called. But it gave me a chance to browse around that particular neighborhood of Vienna. The unimaginable cleanliness of the streets surprised and impressed me. Many boutique stores with clothing for women and men were filled with wonders I had never seen before. Needless to say, I could not even buy a handkerchief for myself. In fascination, I walked from one store to another and stood for a long time in front of each window display with beautifully dressed mannequins, eagerly absorbing every exquisite detail of their dresses and accessories.

It is important to understand that during my life in the Soviet Union, nice, quality things were not readily available in the stores. In order to get nice items—clothes, shoes, and even food—one needed to have some connection with people who worked at the distribution base or with people who could get it from the distribution base and sell it at a higher price. That is why the Vienna stores, my first experience behind the "iron curtain" of the Soviet Union, were a striking discovery of a very different life from the one I'd always known.

***

Christmas in Austria was my first Christmas in December. In the Soviet Union, the New Year was a big holiday for everyone, and Christmas was celebrated by Russian Orthodox on January 7th.

Before Christmas, we went from house to house

along the road to a little town to sell the souvenirs we had brought with us from the Soviet Union. We usually walked in groups of three to four people. The typical items for sale were photo cameras, French perfumes, Russian cutting boards, Russian scarves, and so on. I had only one or two sets of Russian cutting boards for sale.

We knocked at a door. When it opened, we presented our items, explaining, mostly through gestures, that they were splendid gifts. Absolutely amused, Austrians politely looked through the items, often buying some of them—our prices were so cheap that it was hard to resist. We were happy with any amount of money we could make.

Big, fluffy snowflakes were falling and painting white the roads, the slopes of the mountains, and the roofs of the houses. Light smoke calmly drifted from the chimneys. Houses were dressed up with Christmas lights and decorations. The sun was radiant in a clear blue sky above. Silence rang in the air. It was an oasis of serenity.

The two-plus months that I spent in the tranquil and beautiful setting of the Alps mountains in Austria helped me to regain my physical and emotional strength. I was curious and ready to take on whatever would come next.

Austria as I remember it.

Chapter Ten
Italy

Shortly after Christmas, we were transferred to Italy by train. The transit train stopped for 15 minutes at the Vienna railroad station, all the time available for our group of twenty to thirty people to get into the train car with our heavy suitcases. People were not polite or courteous to each other. The families with strong men went to the train car first, while the old and weak were behind. I watched in disbelief. The train car was too high from the platform and I knew I could not lift my suitcases by myself, yet no one was there to help me. I was the last one still standing on the platform. I was ready to cry. I thought I needed to leave my suitcases on the platform and get into the car or I would stay there in Vienna, forever. At the last minute, Irma's teenage son, Daniel, jumped out of the train car and helped me with my suitcases. I will always remember his kindness.

My first impression of Italy was that it was quite dirty and noisy. After I got used to the spotless cleanliness of streets and places in Austria, it disappointed me to see trash on the streets and in public places, along with graffiti. For the first time, I saw homeless people sleeping on rags on the marble floor of the subway in Rome. I also noticed how

Italians get pretty animated when they talk, compared to very restrained Austrian people. But with time, my opinion about Italy changed—I fell in love with the country, and I grew to love the warmth of Italian people. I came to love Italian bread. The Italian language was like music to my ears, and I even learned how to speak some basics.

For the first two weeks in Italy, we were stationed at the bungalow summer camp south of Rome. It was January, and even during the day it was pleasantly warm outside, but at night it was cold. These bungalow houses did not have heat and were not equipped for the wintertime. I remember I was sleeping in my warmest clothes and even covered myself with a mattress from a spare bed in my bungalow. Nevertheless, I got very sick with a cold, so sick that I thought I would not survive it. During the day I walked to the seafront and sat there for long hours—the warm Mediterranean sun and fresh, salty sea air helped me to slowly recover.

After two weeks in the bungalow summer camp, we were told that we needed to rent apartments for ourselves in the nearby city of Torvaianica, a city south of Rome that was founded in the 1940s and is best known for its beaches. It has a population of about 12,700 inhabitants and extends for about eight kilometers along central Lazio's coast. The refugee organization, HIAS, gave us money to cover rent and food. I do not remember the exact amount it was per person, but it was just enough for us not to be on the street dying from hunger. Later on, when I was already in the United States and working, I was required to reimburse HIAS for what they'd spent on me. I paid it back gradually, a small amount each month.

There were plenty of apartments available for rent in January. Many of them were at the seaside. Refugees from the Soviet Union usually shared one apartment—a two-room apartment for two families, a three-room apartment for three families. I was alone and in no way could I afford to pay for a room on my own. Someone from the group introduced me to a young fellow who was traveling alone, too. His actual name completely escapes my memory at present, but I'll call him "Misha."

Misha was in his early twenties. He was very smart and even knew English. For the first time in his life, he was separated from his parents whom he had left behind in the Soviet Union. Misha and I rented a room in the two-room apartment on the first floor of a building at the seaside. We could sit on the balcony and look at the beach and the Mediterranean Sea in front of us. The enormous wardrobe that was in the room divided our room into two halves to give each of us some privacy. Misha was absolutely unprepared for everyday life. He did not know how to manage the little money we had, how to do grocery shopping, or how to cook food. I felt sorry for him and suggested that he contribute some amount of money for food and I would shop and cook for both of us. Misha was happy to do that.

When I went for an interview for the first time in the American Embassy in Rome, I was asked a lot about places I had worked in the Kyzylkum Desert. They had a detailed map of Uzbekistan on the table and asked me about Zarafshan, Navoi, Uchkuduk. I was surprised; I thought they already knew more than I did.

After the first interview, I had to wait for the second one, a very important interview, after which a decision would be made whether to allow my entrance to the United States. Many families were denied the entrance visa to the United States without giving any specific reason or explanation. These people had stayed in Italy for six months, for a year, or even longer. They found some jobs to support themselves and their families. Some of them decided to stay in Italy for good. It was an unsettling time.

Every day at 6:00 p.m., all Soviet refugees who stayed in Torvaianica gathered together at the central square of the city. There were a lot of us, and while I do not know the exact number, I remember how the square was filled with a Russian-speaking crowd, to the amazement of the local population of Italians. We were waiting for the Messenger, usually a man who would stand in the middle of the crowd and read the list of people who had gotten permission to go to America. Even though I had not yet had a second interview in the American Embassy, these daily meetings were the biggest entertainment of the day and a learning experience—people mingled together, told stories, shared news, and made friends.

Misha always found me in the crowd after the announcing part was over and asked, "What's for dinner tonight?" It seemed that he was always hungry. Even though I did not want to go home yet, I felt an obligation to serve him dinner. I thought he was acting like a little baby and since I was not his mother, it was bothering me. There was only one time when I sent Misha to the store to get something for me while I was cooking. He returned with an ice cream cake, our money for two weeks of our food ration gone. We divided the cake among all of the people who lived in both rooms of the apartment. This was the last straw for me. I canceled our contract and let Misha be on his own. Our living arrangements in the apartment remained the same, but I did not cook for him anymore. Meanwhile, we got a new tenant in our room. Another woman, approximately my age, joined us. Three of us shared the room up to the time of my departure.

The distance between Torvaianica and Rome was about 40 kilometers (25 miles), and there was bus transportation. I used the bus a few times. The ride was about 50 to 60 minutes. I did not go often, because the bus was usually packed with people and reminded me very much of the buses in the Soviet Union. Also, traveling by bus cost money I could not spare. Very soon I learned I could get to Rome by hitchhiking—every car driven by an Italian man would stop when they saw a young, pretty woman hitchhiking on the road. Several times I even hitchhiked with Misha. When the car stopped, I told the driver that he was my brother. I must say that most of the time Italians were very reckless drivers, and I felt uncomfortable in the car quite often.

I loved my outings to Rome. I enjoyed exploring the beautiful city where every stone has a history. Once or twice a month, all museums in Rome were free and I took advantage of this. Visiting the Colosseum, St. Peter's Basilica, the museums of the Vatican, including the Sistine Chapel and the Trevi

Fountain, to name a few, all became unforgettable experiences and cultural enrichment for me.

On the days when I was not traveling to Rome, I was discovering Torvaianica. Some items and events from my time there will be engraved in my memory forever.

For instance, there was a shoe and leather accessories store across from our apartment. In the Soviet Union, Italian shoes and leather accessories always were part of every woman's desirable outfit, but they were difficult to get. In the store across the street was everything I could only dream about: elegant leather shoes, hand purses, belts. I visited the store quite often—not to buy, just to look. The store seemed to me big and exceptional. Years later, in 2001, Sparky and I traveled to Italy and visited Torvaianica. We found the beachfront apartment where I lived at the beginning of 1990 and a shoe store across the road. To my amusement, all at once, I saw an ordinary little store that I calmly browsed through—it did not give me the excitement that it had in 1990. Perception is everything, and I was a very different person by 2001.

The main drag of Torvaianica with its famous Italian bakeries, restaurants, and shopping sprawled along the Mediterranean coast. On the snuggly, warm Italian evenings of January and February, I liked to stroll the street, window shopping and people watching. Italian people did not like to hold back their emotions—they laughed, they talked loudly, helping themselves with gestures, and I loved the music of the Italian language. I always stopped at the window of one particular bakery to examine all of the wonderful baked goods on display, though I could not afford to buy any. One of these baked goods was filled with a mix of rich semolina and ricotta cheese, and was a shell-shaped pastry called Sfogliatelle; Zeppole was another pastry consisting of a deep-fried dough ball dusted with powdered sugar and sometimes filled with various sweets; there was also biscotti, Venetian cookies, and hot chocolate cake—I could not take my eyes off of these beautiful culinary arts. One evening, the owner of the store, a middle-aged Italian man wearing a white chef's coat and hat, with a lush body, dark mustache, and kind, laughing eyes, came out carrying a plate with a few biscotti and Venetian cookies and offered it to me to taste. Bewildered by his offer and the fact that he, probably, had been watching me the evening after evening in front of his window, I did not have the strength to refuse his marvelous-looking, tasty Italian pastries.

Finally, the day came when I received a letter from the American Embassy in Rome with the invitation for the second and most important interview of my life. As I struggled with the English language then, I clearly understood the date and time of my interview, but I completely missed the location. Besides, I was pretty sure that there was only one location for the American Embassy in Rome and I knew where it was. But I was wrong.

The interview was scheduled for 12:00 p.m. I wanted to be collected and prepared. To eliminate any possibility of being late, I arrived at the American Embassy in Rome at 11:00 a.m. It was a sunny, beautiful, spring-like day; I lost myself for a short time (while waiting) on the fascinating streets of

Rome. The sidewalk cafes were full of business people enjoying their lunch hours. I was thinking, "Is there going to be a time in my life when I, like them, can sit leisurely at a sidewalk cafe and have lunch? And feel myself as confident, relaxed, and happy as these people?" I wanted to believe that this time would eventually come during my life.

About 11:45 a.m., I returned to the American Embassy expecting to soon be called by the guard. There was a good crowd of people waiting, like me, to be called. One by one they went inside until only I was left waiting. It was after 12:00 p.m. I got anxious—I began to wonder why I was not being called. I showed my paper to the guard. He explained to me (mostly by gestures and with some Italian phrases) that my interview was in a completely different location on the other side of the city. I was shocked. First, I had no money to get a taxi. Second, I thought my life was doomed. With this realization, I stood on the curb of the street in the center of Rome and sobbed bitterly. Tears rolled down my face.

Well, the Italian people did not easily tolerate this scene. Soon enough, a taxi cab stopped by me. The driver got out of the car and asked me what had happened. Continuing to cry, I showed him my paper invitation for the interview and tried to explain to him that I had come to the wrong location. He looked at the paper and then at me and started vigorously gesticulating, pushing me inside the taxi cab. Even inside the taxi, I could not stop crying. The driver turned around to me shouting some equivalent of "Shut up" in Italian. I became quiet. I realized he was going to drive me to the address where I needed to be.

While he was driving, I feverishly thought about how I would pay for my ride as I had very little money in my pocket. But I was wearing a gorgeous silver ring with a gemstone on the ring finger of my left hand. The ring was handmade with an intricate Gothic design and a big, beautiful, pink, tourmaline stone—it was my favorite ring! I bought it during my vacation in Latvia, a country on the Baltic Sea—Latvia was a part of the Soviet Union from 1940 to 1991. I immediately decided to pay for my ride with the ring.

We arrived at the address of the second location of the American Embassy. I paid for the ride with the ring. The grounds of the Embassy were surrounded by a high fence and the gates were closed. I was not sure how I could get inside. However, the gates opened for an incoming car and I just sneaked through the gates behind the car and ran towards the main building. I entered a room full of people waiting to be called for their interviews. My face was red, mascara smeared across my face, and my hair was messed up. Immediately, I heard my name being called. I walked into a smaller room where two men asked me questions. Then one man with reddish hair said to me how he had grown up in Buffalo, New York. He asked me if I knew how severe the winter could be in Buffalo. I said, "Probably not worse than in Siberia." They both laughed. With this, my interview was over. From that point, I would have to wait for the Messenger at the Torvaianica square to call my name and give me an official paper with "Yes" or "No" written on it.

After two weeks or so, the Messenger at the 6:00 p.m. gathering at the Torvaianica square called my name. I was not nervous; for some reason, I was sure that it would be "Yes". I calmly opened the envelope—there were dates for my flight from Rome to New York City. It was exciting news for me, and in anticipation of big changes in my life, I started to prepare myself for the trip.

Torvaianica, Italy. "We could sit on the balcony and look at the beach and the Mediterranean Sea"

Chapter Eleven
Buffalo

I landed in New York City, at the John F. Kennedy International Airport, on the morning of March 15, 1990. A representative of HIAS met me and some other Soviet refugees who were on my flight. He gave me a ticket for the flight to Buffalo, New York, and showed me where to wait for the flight. A Jewish organization in Buffalo had agreed to be my sponsor. By that time, my cousin Rimma, with her husband Yury and little daughter Elina, were already in Buffalo. They had arrived a few months before me.

On the flight to Buffalo, I was chatting (mostly with gestures) with a young Black woman sitting next to me. She was with a little baby girl. As I understood, they were refugees from Africa. The baby was crying all the time, and I was trying to hold the baby and comfort her.

No one met me upon my arrival in Buffalo. It was evening, and I did not know what to do, where to go, or where I was going to spend my first night in America. Seeing my confusion, the Black, African woman from the flight kindly invited me to spend a night with them. Since I had no other options, I accepted. We arrived at an old two-floor house with many Black families inside. Each family had a room, and they shared the kitchen and the bathroom of the house. A lot of small kids were running around. They were all refugees from some African country. The house, inside and outside, was in pretty run-down condition. It surprised me, as it was not at all what I expected to see in the United States. But I was thankful that they gave me a corner where I could put my head down after a very long and thrilling first day in America. In the morning, using the phone in the house, I called my cousin Rimma, and they picked me up.

On that same day, I met with the representative of the Buffalo Jewish organization. Her name was Larissa. She took me to the apartment they had already rented for me. It was a one-bedroom on Delaware Avenue in Buffalo, with the living room, bedroom, kitchen, and bathroom on the second floor. The apartment was furnished with everything that one might need: dishes, utensils, pots and pans, towels, linens, etc. Soon two men brought and unpacked furniture: a bedroom set, table, loveseat, and even a little TV. The furniture was brand new, delivered right from the store. I was absolutely shocked and amazed at the same time. Again, tears were rolling down my face, but this time they were happy tears. I could not understand why so much care was taken for me without asking for anything in return. In the Soviet Union, people waited for years to get their own apartment, yet in the United States, I had just arrived and everything was ready for me, all prepared with such thoughtfulness. I was overwhelmed by everything that was happening around me and by my feelings. I needed time to sort things out. Later in the evening, I turned on my little brand-new TV and I was horrified: I heard the sound but could not tell one word from another. I was sitting on my new bed in my own apartment and thinking, "What did I do? How am I going to survive here?!" My first night in my apartment was sleepless. The unknown new life frightened me, and I knew that I would have to overcome all of the challenges, no matter how difficult they would be.

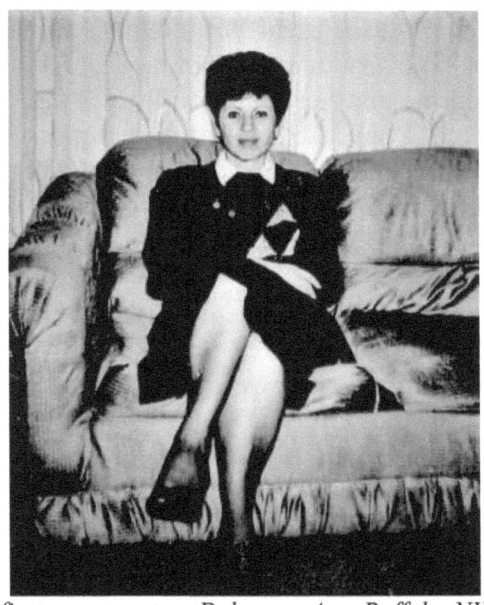

In my first apartment on Delaware Ave, Buffalo, NY, 1990.

The next morning I found a library. I got tapes for learning English. From that point forward, whenever I was doing something at home, I ran these tapes over and over again, repeating, "Hello, my name is…" and "How do you do?" I knew that learning English was the most important thing in my life. Soon I started to attend a school where I learned English as a second language.

The first thing I took care of, when I settled in my new apartment, was filling out all of the papers necessary to bring Natasha to the States. At that point, Natasha was already working as a nurse in the Yalta hospital. I knew that waiting could take several years. As soon as I started to work, I began sending her packages with clothes. During our three-year-long separation, Natasha sent me letters, full of love, expressing in every one of them how much she loved and missed me and her gratitude for the packages she got from me. I have kept all of these letters for thirty years. I read them over recently, and I thought, "Wow, how much things have changed in thirty years. Why?" I do not have an answer to this question.

Across from my apartment was Hills, a discount department store. It existed until 1999, when it was acquired by Ames. This was the first department store I visited in the United States. I needed to buy something to use in my kitchen. I remember that when I walked into the store, the abundance and variety of merchandise shocked me. The security guard, an Italian man in his sixties named Bruno, noticed my confusion and asked if he could help me. Somehow I explained to him what I was looking for and he took me to the correct aisle. After that day, he recognized me and greeted me with a big smile every time he was on duty when I came to shop. We became friends for many years. Once in a while, he would come to visit me in my apartment across from the store at the end of his shift with a bottle of good Italian wine. He listened to my stories in broken

English and told me his. We laughed a lot. But after my first shopping experience in Hills, for months, I preferred to go to the store later at night (the store was open 24 hours), when there were fewer people and I could go from aisle to aisle and learn and touch all of the things they sold there. To tell the truth, even now, thirty years later, I still prefer discount department stores to upscale ones.

Since I did not have a car (I never drove a car in the Soviet Union), for the first four to five months in Buffalo, I walked everywhere I needed to go. It was strange for me not to see people walking outside, just cars passing by. I thought to myself, "Where am I going to meet American people?" Another strange thing for me was that if I occasionally met somebody walking in our neighborhood, they always smiled and said "Hello" as if they had known me for years. I learned that to say "Hi" to strangers was a part of American culture, although it was not true for big cities like New York City. But during the first eight years of my time spent in Buffalo, I learned about my new life from everything I encountered there.

I passed the driving test after being in the country for three or four months. It was an extremely stressful experience for me—with all of the tasks unfamiliar to me, I also needed to overcome the enormous language barrier. I failed the first time, and the second time I passed, but I was so stressed out that I forgot my handbag with all of my documents in the car they used to give me the test. Luckily, my handbag was returned to me later and nothing was missing from it.

The beginning of my new life in America was stressful, amazing, and unpredictable—all at once. I tried to learn and absorb all of the unknowns that surrounded me. I was determined to keep a spark of life alive inside of me and share it with others.

Niagara Falls near Buffalo, NY, view from Canadian side.

Chapter Twelve
Burger King

The Jewish Federation of Greater Buffalo sponsored us, the Soviet refugees. They helped us through every step of our new life. They paid for my apartment for four months and provided me with some money for food. After four months, we were supposed to be on our own terms financially. The Jewish organization and the synagogues of Northern Buffalo were places where we could all meet for holiday events, lectures, or even to see a movie.

The first movie I watched in America was in the synagogue, and it was *Fiddler on the Roof*. In the Soviet Union, I had read the book by Sholem Aleichem and watched the Russian version—Tevye the Milkman—which was released in 1985, fourteen years after the original American movie. What shocked me was how different the American movie was from the Soviet one. The major distinction was in how Jewish people were portrayed in the American movie as a freedom-loving, proud, strong nation, while in the Soviet movie, I always sensed a grain of pettiness towards Jewish people. *Fiddler on the Roof* gave me such joy that I burst into tears.

That is when I met Marvin. Marvin was a well-dressed Jewish man in his late seventies. He was a true gentleman. I do not think he was ever married.

Marvin asked me why I was crying and I tried to explain it to him. After the movie was over, he offered me a ride home.

My friend Marvin, Buffalo, NY, 1990.

After that evening, Marvin became like a father figure to me. He drove me around Buffalo, showed me places, and took me out to dinner. One evening he took me out for dinner, and when the waitress brought the check, Marvin discovered he had forgotten his wallet at home. However, since he was a frequent customer in that restaurant, everybody knew him by name. He just said to the waitress that he would be right back. We drove to his house to pick up his wallet and came back to pay. For me, the experience was unheard of; it amused me so much that to this day, I still remember it like it happened just yesterday. Marvin was always there for me when I needed help. He was the one who took me to the manager of the Burger King fast-food restaurant at the corner of Delaware Street, near my apartment building. He said to the manager, "This young lady needs a job." That is how I got my first job in America—I cleared tables and washed dishes at Burger King.

One day, Marvin brought Robert to Burger King. Robert was a tall man in his forties, with sad eyes behind thick glasses. He looked like a big baby. Robert was Marvin's neighbor who lived alone, across the street. Marvin told me that Robert was looking for someone to clean his house, and they wondered if I would be interested in doing that job. Of course, I was interested! That is how I got my second job: cleaning Robert's house. It was an old house of a bachelor, dusty, with outdated furniture. While I was cleaning, Robert sat in a big chair and watched me. Sometimes he would go down to the basement and bring up some old dish or vase to show me—with a sadness in his voice, he explained that these items had belonged to his parents who had passed away. When I came to clean his house the second or third time, Robert asked me to marry him. His proposition frightened me, and I said "no". I could not imagine myself living in that house with dusty old furniture, a basement full of aged articles, and a big, sad baby-man. We remained on good terms, and I kept cleaning his house for a while after that day.

Later on, when I was no longer working for him, Robert got married to a Russian woman who came for a visit from Ukraine. Her name was Nadya. One day I met Robert in the store and he told me he loved his married life. I believe that Robert and Nadya are still happily living together today in his house in Buffalo.

One day I learned that my dear friend Marvin quietly passed away during his sleep at night. It was very sad news for me—I lost someone who cared about me and made a difference in my life. Marvin will forever remain alive in my heart and memory.

I was cleaning people's houses for quite a long time. That is how I survived the time when I was going to school, taking classes in college, and studying for two years to be an X-ray technician.

Chapter Thirteen
Calumet Arts Cafe

One hot summer day, I got a call from the Jewish Center—someone wanted to interview me for a job. When asked if I was interested, I said, "Of course." Shortly after, I got a call from a man. His name was Mark Goldman, Buffalo historian, and a local hero to some; he had been instrumental in the revitalization of the Chippewa Street area. Mark had a plan to transform Chippewa Street in downtown Buffalo from, what many people described as a red-light district, into an entertainment center of the city. He purchased the Calumet Building in 1988. By 1990, he was ready to open a restaurant in the Calumet Building, and he was hiring people.

I do not remember how I talked with him on the phone—at that point in my life I was terrified every time the phone rang and I heard something in English. I had a hard time understanding it and communicating. But when Mark Goldman called, I had no choice, and I was trying my best to communicate well. Mark invited me for an interview, but I did not yet have a car. He thought for a minute and told me he would come to my apartment to interview me.

There was no air conditioner in my apartment. Summers in Buffalo could be hot and muggy. It was one of these summer days, and the temperature in my apartment was quite uncomfortable when Mark arrived and introduced himself. He looked around to assess the situation.

He asked, "Where is your fan?"

I said, "I do not have one yet."

He looked at me curiously and asked, "Isn't it hot for you?"

"Yes," I said, "but I can tolerate it."

Then, Mark said, "I'll be back," and he disappeared through my door. Fifteen minutes later he came back with a huge fan he proudly hoisted in the middle of my room, and then he started his interview. He had bought the fan in the hardware store on the first floor of my apartment building. I was absolutely astounded by this act of generosity from a stranger. I used this fan for a long time, and later on, when I did not need it anymore, I still kept it and even took it with me when I moved away from Buffalo. When I got married to Sparky and moved to Virginia from my apartment in Maryland, the fan traveled with me. I kept it in the basement of Sparky's house for many years, and only when we were remodeling the basement did Sparky suggest it was time to get rid of it. Soon after that, Sparky and I went for a visit to Buffalo, and we met Mark Goldman there. The first thing he asked me was if I still had his fan.

But back to the interview in my apartment. Mark Goldman offered me a job in his restaurant, "Calumet Arts Cafe," waiting on tables. I was so excited. I quit my job at Burger King and started to work in the "Calumet Arts Cafe" at night after school. The restaurant with live music became a very popular place for the Buffalo elite and intellectuals. I loved my work. I learned about American life and the American people there. However, my English was still not very good, and often I did not understand what my customers were asking. One case I still remember was how a woman asked me to bring an ashtray to her table. I did not know what the word "ashtray" meant. I ran back to the kitchen and asked feverishly, "What is an ashtray?" My coworkers laughed and explained it to me.

When my cousin Marik from Moscow came to visit us in Buffalo, I asked Mark Goldman to give him any kind of job in the "Calumet Arts Cafe". It was at the beginning of 1990s when the Soviet Union had just collapsed. In Russia, it was a time of a political crisis, serious disorder, and economic chaos. The living standards for average citizens dropped drastically, even though they never were too high before in the Soviet Union. My cousin Marik wanted to make some money during his visit to us that he could bring back to his family. He washed dishes in the "Calumet Arts Cafe" for several weeks and made some money before he went back to Moscow. Marik passed away on April 1, 2015, from a long battle with cancer; he was put to rest in Moscow.

Mark Goldman, his generosity to me and my family, and my work in his "Calumet Arts Cafe" will stay in my memory forever, as well as my gratitude to Mark for his help when I just started my new life and needed any kind of help and support.

Mark Goldman and I, Buffalo, NY, 1995.

Chapter Fourteen
Greeley Street

After being in my first apartment on Delaware Street for four months, I moved to the first floor of a little house on Greeley Street. The house was old and small, but cozy. I installed new wallpaper in the kitchen, painted walls in the bathroom, and put in new window treatments. Soon it became my home sweet home. The owner of the house was Rose Marie, a widow who lived in a nice house in North Buffalo. She had three adult children from her first husband, who was Armenian. Her second, Indian husband, was a doctor who had passed away. Rose Marie was (and still is) a very interesting person. She traveled to faraway countries where she taught English and helped those who had been deprived of their human rights. We became friends, and our friendship continues at present.

Rose Marie moved to Boulder, Colorado, around 1998 and still lives there. In November 2004, Sparky and I visited her in Boulder. She took us to dinner at the Boulder Dushanbe Teahouse. Its hand-carved and hand-painted ceiling, tables, stools, columns, and exterior ceramic panels had been made in the sister city of Dushanbe, the capital of Tajikistan, and shipped to Boulder. Tajikistan and Dushanbe in particular, are very familiar to me as I had my first summer internship from the Geological College in the expedition at the Pamir Mountains near Dushanbe. There I was badly bitten by the Akbash dog that guards sheep in the mountains.

Rose Marie and I in Boulder, Colorado, in the Dushanbe Teahouse, 2004.

At that time, Tajikistan was (and still is) a small, mountainous country in Central Asia, lying side by side with Afghanistan. It was one of the republics of the Soviet Union. This was a land where one could feel the breath of the romance of oriental fairy tales and the Great Silk Road. In Dushanbe, people immediately understood that they were in the East. All women wore bright trousers and tunics, and colorful scarves were wrapped around their heads. Dushanbe was a pleasant city: mature Plane trees growing on both sides of the streets created green canopies that, even in the hot summer, maintained a comfortable climate; people were friendly. Another attraction of Dushanbe was an amazing market with an abundance of local produce such as nuts, dried and fresh fruit, vegetables, meat, spices, and Tajik-style round bread—"*лепешка*". The most striking and unforgettable for me were two items in the Dushanbe market: pyramids of yellow melons—enormous, oblong and pointy at the ends like an American football; also piles of grapes called "Ladies fingers"—one of the most ancient and delicious grape varieties, which got its name from the elongated shape of the berries. The Tajik-style round bread with "Ladies fingers" grapes always made an excellent lunch.

The Tajik-style round bread in Dushanbe, Tajikistan.

"Ladies fingers" grapes in Dushanbe, Tajikistan.

Yellow melons in Dushanbe, Tajikistan.

Another reason why I remember and love Dushanbe even now is because my love story with Nikolai Gelya started there.

Nikolai had just graduated from the same college that I was in and got his first job in a different geological expedition not far from Dushanbe. It was a tradition for all of us youngsters who worked in the geological expeditions around Dushanbe—to descend from the mountains and to meet in one particular restaurant in Dushanbe on Friday evenings to start a weekend of fun. I remember how I walked into the restaurant and felt someone's gaze on me. I looked up and, sure enough, a handsome young fellow with big greenish eyes was looking right at me. When our eyes met, he smiled at me, looking friendly, and I smiled back. He made sure to take a seat next to me at the dinner table. We talked, we laughed, we danced until it was way past midnight. Then we wandered around the sleeping city until morning, talking about ourselves and everything else in the world. After this day, we couldn't wait for the next weekend to come. When I was in the hospital after being bitten by the Akbash dog, Nikolai came to visit me. When summer and my internship were over, I had to return to Kiev, but at this point we decided that we were going to be together. Nikolai was transferred to work in the Kyzylkum Desert, and I joined him there just before New Year's Day, 1969.

Back to the house on Greeley Street. Next to my little house was a house similar to mine. A woman named Alla (the same name as my sister) and her husband Sam lived there. Both of them had been doctors in Ukraine. Even though they were about ten years older than I was, Alla and I developed a powerful bond. It was a gift to have neighbors that were members of my community, people with whom I could talk, go for walks in the evening, or get help or advice from when I needed it.

One day I got a call from the CIA. The voice on the other end of the line informed me they wanted to interview me about my work in the Kyzylkum Desert. It frightened me—I had dealt with the KGB in the Soviet Union and I did not want to deal with any similar organization in the United States.

When a young man in a gray suit arrived at the house, he asked me questions for three hours, all about uranium and gold deposits in the Kyzylkum Desert. He was very polite. Of course, my English was still very limited. Even so, three hours of questioning was a long time. I wondered what would happen next. To my relief, after that day, they never bothered me again.

One day I called the Family Reunification organization to find out Natasha's status. I was told that her application was denied and that she was not eligible for the program because her father was not Jewish. They told me she might never be allowed to enter the United States. I could not believe what I had just heard. I shook like a leaf. I cried in my little house so loudly that my neighbors ran to help me. They worried about me. My shock was so strong and devastating, I could not stop crying. I thought that my life in the United States would not make any sense if I could not bring my only child to be with me. From that day on, I started to fight for my daughter. I spent many months writing letters to various refugee organizations and other offices, visiting officials and synagogues in Buffalo and elsewhere. My neighbor and friend, Alla, helped me. We went together to talk with the rabbi in the synagogue. The rabbi wrote a letter that stated that according to Jewish law, a child in the mixed marriage born from a Jewish mother was considered to be Jewish, too. I sent this letter to the Family Reunification organization. Nothing seemed to improve the situation.

The Jewish Center gave me the name of the best

immigration lawyer in Buffalo. He agreed to give me the first consultation for free. I went to see him. I told him I did not have any money to pay him (at that time he charged $200 per hour), but I could cook for him and bring him freshly prepared delicious food when we had an appointment. He felt my pain and was kind enough to accept my proposition. Soon after, he started to work on Natasha's case. It took several years for him to do this. Every time I came to see him, I brought along a big bag of freshly cooked and baked food from my Russian-Ukrainian-Uzbek cuisines. He loved to eat, and he seemed to love my food. He would rub his hands and say, "Smells good!" He ended up filing an Affidavit of Support for Natasha and sent it to Moscow—he was ready to be her sponsor. He asked me not to show anyone this paper because he disclosed all of his finances on it.

Before we sent the Affidavit to Moscow, Natasha was denied an entry visa to the United States three times. After we sent the Affidavit, she suddenly got permission to enter the country as a refugee under the Family Reunification program. I was so happy and grateful to hear this news. Natasha arrived in America in January 1993, via a flight from Moscow to New York City. I will remember forever the kindness of a man who took a case without being paid for it and was ready to sponsor my daughter.

Kindness is helping the world, one person at a time.

Chapter Fifteen
Schools

The first school I went to in America was to learn English as a second language. Then I went to a special school for adult Americans who had never finished high school and wanted to get a GED (General Educational Development) diploma. There were a good number of Russian immigrants in this school because the school promised to help with job placement. I remember one of the lessons they taught us was how to dress properly, both in general and for interviews. It seemed very bizarre to us, Russian immigrants—most of us had been highly educated in the Soviet Union and worked there as doctors, teachers, engineers, and so on. We were interested only in learning English, but we had to follow the rules of the school. After I completed this school and my English improved, I took a certified nursing assistant (CNA) course—I needed to get work as soon as possible, and the course required only a few months of study and then an exam for the certification.

No matter what school I was going to, I was always an outstanding student. In general, I love to learn. I successfully completed the CNA course and passed an exam. I was extremely proud when I got my first certificate in America. I got a job in a nursing home as a nurse assistant for the night shift. To tell the truth, I absolutely cannot function properly working at night and had never worked a night shift in my life. But I had no choice—the night shift was the only one available, and I was grateful that I could get it. It was hard, and not only because I was working at night. My responsibilities were to clean and turn over old, bedridden patients. There was a strong, mixed odor of urine, feces, and sweat in the rooms. It was the smell of the end of life. On the patients' nightstands and on the walls were pictures from when they were young and full of life. They resembled nothing of what they had once been. It was very depressing.

After working there for several months, I thought, "I can get a better job than this." So, I went to college to learn how to be a medical assistant, a professional who supports the work of physicians. There I enjoyed all medical subjects and earned very good grades on them. Only one subject was a complete nightmare for me: typing. It required me to put on headphones, listen to the tape, and type what I heard at a speed of 35 words per minute, using all ten fingers properly. By virtue of my English limitations, it was an almost impossible task. But I told myself, "Nothing is impossible. Just practice." And I practiced. I bought a keyboard for typing and practiced for hours at home. In the end, I passed the exam. And I'm so glad I did—the skill of typing was very beneficial to me when I was working as a computer programmer later on, and even as I spent time writing this book.

After being in the medical assistant course for a year, I realized that when I finished it and started to work, I would not make enough money to support myself. I thought about what I could do next. I knew I needed to secure a job that would give me enough money to be on my own and survive. After some research, I decided to apply to Buffalo Millard Fillmore Hospital's X-ray school, a two-year program. Upon completion and successful passing of a certification exam, I could become a radiology technologist, the person who performs X-rays on patients. I thought it was as close to my previous profession of geophysicist as it could be—I had learned about physics and radiation before. In addition, the pay rate for X-ray techs was substantially higher than that of medical assistants. It didn't hurt that X-ray techs were in high demand at the time.

During my first application attempt, I was not accepted, most likely due to my English limitations. So I waited one more year and applied again. This time I was accepted. The school was structured so that we were in classes for three days and working on the floor helping X-ray techs and gaining actual skills during the other two days. At 42 years old, I think I was the oldest student in the class, as most of my classmates enrolled right after high school. I maintained good grades. I must say that my academic achievements were better than practical. I always liked to learn new subjects. During my years in the X-ray school, 1992–1994, I was very busy learning during the week and cleaning houses on the weekends in order to support myself.

After I graduated from X-ray school and successfully passed the certification exam, I started job hunting. It was not easy to find a job in Buffalo, especially when I was looking for my first professional job. All I could get was part-time work, with no benefits. In the beginning, I had two jobs in different doctor's offices. Later on, I worked with a mobile X-ray company. It was a night shift, again. I needed to drive a minivan with a heavy mobile X-ray machine inside and go from one nursing home to another, take an X-ray, return to the office to develop the film, and take it to the doctor's house so that he could read it.

It was especially hard during the winter. Buffalo may as well own winter. The season's first snowfall usually arrives in November, and the last snowfall typically happens in April. Over half of the annual snowfall comes from the "lake-effect" process. Lake-effect snow occurs when the relatively warm water of Lake Erie crosses with cold air. The air becomes saturated, creating clouds and precipitation—snow bands. A snow band's location is always determined by wind direction. Areas south of Buffalo are usually prone to receive much more lake-effect snow than locations to the north. I remember that so many times my pager would beep when Severe Weather Alerts were announced on the radio, and a travel ban went into effect for the entire Buffalo region. I was dispatched even when roads were completely covered with inches of snow and slush with icy patches. To drive around Buffalo and the suburbs alone at night in wintertime, with frequent snowstorms, was a nightmare job for me, but I was paid $30 per hour, so I was determined to keep it as long as I could. In addition, several days per week I worked during the day in the doctor's office. It was a tough life, but I never expected that it would be easy.

Chapter Sixteen
Natasha's Arrival

At long last, Natasha arrived in the United States in 1993. I went to New York City to meet her at the airport. I was extremely happy—three long years of our separation, worries, uncertainty—all of these ended as we started a new era. We needed to decide how she was going to learn English and what to do with her profession—should she go to school again and get a nursing diploma? We had to figure out how she could make some money and many other "how" questions. The good thing was she was still young, and it is always easier to adjust to a new life as a young person. There was a sizable community of immigrants from the Soviet Union in Buffalo, so in a short time, Natasha made friends. I introduced her to my clients for whom I had been cleaning houses for several years, so Natasha could make some money, too. Even though life was still hard for us, there was some happiness in it. I felt I had accomplished the most important mission of my life—I had brought my daughter to the free country. She now had so many opportunities in front of her. Her life would become very different.

Even Natasha had a job in Yalta before she left, but the salary was so low and the cost of living so high that it was hard to make ends meet. She lived in a tiny room without windows and without a bathroom.

Getting her own apartment in Yalta was an impossible task. The Soviet Union had already collapsed and brought hardship, chaos, and unpredictability to everyone's lives.

The Jewish Center of Buffalo, my sponsor and my help, introduced me to an American woman, Marilyn. The purpose was to help me assimilate faster into my new life and speed up my English learning process. Marilyn was around my age, maybe a little younger, and single. We became friendly; she took me for lunch every once in a while. Marilyn worked at the Research Institute of Addictions. She told me about this nice, very polite fellow, with whom she was working, named Brian. Brian was single and unattached and Marilyn asked if I wanted to introduce him to Natasha. I asked Natasha about it. She said no, that she did not want to have any arranged introductions. I reasoned with her, "You are in a new country. It is better to meet someone who is known to our friend. It never hurts to try. If you do not like him, you do not need to see him again." Natasha finally agreed and Marilyn arranged for a day and time with Brian.

When Brian showed up at our house for the first time, I had to translate to Natasha what he was saying because Natasha had just started to learn English and her vocabulary was limited to a few words. For some reason, Brian was nervous and sweating. But to my surprise, the relationship between Natasha and Brian continued to develop after their first date. It was not long before Natasha moved in with Brian, into his apartment. She also was accepted to the nursing school for a two-year program. They lived together for four years before they eventually got married.

Natasha was set to marry Brian in Buffalo, New York on July 27, 1997. We invited Nikolai to the wedding. He had a hard time getting his visitation visa from Uzbekistan to the United States, and he arrived late. He stayed in Buffalo for about a month. It was the first time after many years that we had seen each other, and we talked a lot. I was working a few days a week in the store in the mall at Niagara Falls at that time, and he even went there with me. He walked through the mall while I worked. I'm sure he felt the same cultural shock and astonishment as I had when I first arrived in the United States and visited Hills department store in Buffalo.

Natasha and Brian, Buffalo, NY, July 27, 1997.

After my working hours, we drove home together. For us, it was another chance to have a genuine conversation. The day he left for Uzbekistan is a vivid memory for me forever. Nikolai did not want to leave, but to keep him in the United States was impossible—he had neither legal permission nor the money to stay illegally and jump through the hoops to get legal status. We were also struggling, so we could not help him. At that time, I knew he was divorced from Olga, his second wife. What I did not know and he did not tell me was how he was living with a woman named Galina in Uchkuduk—we found out about her when she sent us a letter later on. I felt he expected some miracle to happen and he would stay in the United States. He did not want to go back, and it was his last hope. I remember his eyes when we took him to the airport to say the last goodbye—they were full of yearning and sadness. We heard later on that when Nikolai landed in Uzbekistan, all of the gifts he had brought from the United States were confiscated in customs, and he was detained and then thrown into jail. We do not know how long he was in jail and how he got out of it—we did not have any contact with him. I suspect he had to pay a bribe in order to get out. Perhaps Galina helped him to arrange that. Uzbekistan always was and probably still is a very corrupt country.

Natasha and Nikolai Gelya on jet ski, lake Erie, Buffalo, NY, 1997.

Approximately one year after his visit to us, Nikolai Gelya retired in Uchkuduk, Uzbekistan. As part of the retirement program, he got an apartment in the city of Poltava in Ukraine where he moved with Galina. For those people who worked for many years in the industry and were retiring, a special arrangement with apartments in Russia or Ukraine was available as a part of the retirement package. It made sense because the little city in the middle of the desert was built to provide for the needs of working people and could not offer anything for the lifestyle of the retired workers. The arid climate of the desert would have added a very negative effect to a person who would spend his retirement years there, too.

The 1990s were very strenuous years for the country we came from, as chaos ruled everywhere. In 1998, an economic austerity program was begun in

Ukraine, which was based on a sharp cut in government spending. It was triggered by the Southeast Asia economic collapse. International investors had begun to quit the Ukrainian treasury bond market, increasing concerns of a looming financial crisis in the country. In Ukraine, Nikolai could not get his pension money because he worked in Uzbekistan. Since the Soviet Union collapsed in 1991, Ukraine and Uzbekistan became two separate countries with ever-changing sets of laws. There was also a shortage of food, and Nikolai had to work as a night watchman for the store. It was at that time for Nikolai when his alcohol addiction became the only way to reduce the stress and escape the dreadful reality around him. We knew very little of his and Galina's life together in Poltava, Ukraine, since letters from Nikolai came to us very rarely.

Chapter Seventeen
My Friends

Friendships that I developed during my first years in Buffalo helped me to go through all the ups and downs of my life. I came across many people with whom I developed some kind of relationship, but with four of my best friends I have kept in touch for all these passing years. I'm forever grateful for their presence in my life, for their support and inspiration. They will always have a special place in my heart.

I met Sofiya in the first school I attended to learn English in 1990. Sofiya had arrived in Buffalo from Italy on May 7, 1990, with her parents. They were from Minsk, Belarus, and, like me, they went through Austria and Italy before they came to the United States as refugees. Her father soon passed away, but her mother, Busya, lived until she was 94 years old. Busya was a wise and kind person. When I was in distress, their house was always a healing place for my soul. Busya never failed to offer something delicious to eat and to warm my heart.

I met Tanya in 1993, soon after she arrived in Buffalo from Minsk, Belarus, with her two adult children. Her husband had passed away in Minsk just before they left. Natasha became friends with Dima, Tanya's son. When Dima once came to our house on Greeley Street, I asked him about his mom and told him to bring her to us one day. That's how we met, and since then, Tanya and I had maintained a very special bond throughout the years. Even now, I miss talking with Tanya daily.

Alla and Sam were my neighbors on Greeley Street. They had reached the United States the same way I did: through Austria and Italy, but they arrived one year earlier. Alla and Sam were from Ukraine and had worked as doctors there. In Buffalo, they had two twin sons with their families and a lot of other relatives. After spending a few years in the United States, their sons returned to Russia and Ukraine and built successful businesses there. At present, Alla and Sam live in New York City.

I met Lenny in Sofiya's house around 1991, and we have been friends all these years since. Lenny's husband, Dr. Park, was a very successful and well-known eye doctor in the Buffalo area. They had several offices, and Lenny ran the business part. Eventually, their offices closed. They also divorced later on.

In May 1995, when I got my U.S. citizenship, Lenny threw a big celebration party for me in her beautiful Buffalo house. When Lenny went on a trip to Israel in 1997, she made a special tour to the Northern District of Israel to visit my father in Nazareth Illit and say "hello" to him for me. Later on, Lenny sold her house in Buffalo and moved to the Washington, D.C. area to take college courses. When I moved from Buffalo to the Washington, D.C. area to look for a job, I lived with Lenny for two to three months before I could rent my own place. Then Lenny got a job in California. After spending several years in California, Lenny moved to the east coast of Florida for her retirement years.

At the time I'm writing this book—the time of the COVID-19 pandemic and Trump's disastrous presidency, when there are fewer than four weeks left before the election and Trump got infected with COVID-19—my relationship with all of my Russian best friends, Tanya, Sofiya, Alla, is in the quite broken stage. We have drifted apart a lot due to the fact that they are "Trumpers" and we cannot even discuss political issues. I do not understand how they all recognized very well the totalitarian regime of the Soviet Union and now Russia and other republics, but they do not see that Trump is craving the same kind of rules here, in the United States. They do not see that Trump is a threat to our democracy and to our country. They do not see that he is a crook, a criminal, and a liar. It makes me very sad.

Tanya (left), I, Busya and Lenny, Buffalo, NY, 1995.

Sofiya, Buffalo, NY, 2006.

Alla, Buffalo, NY, 2006.

Chapter Eighteen
Dot-Com Bubble

The dot-com bubble was a stock market bubble caused by excessive speculation in Internet-related companies. In the late 1990s, the euphoria of online commerce and services began. Many Internet companies (known as "dot-coms") were launched. Assumptions were made that online companies were going to be worth millions. At the end of the 1990s, the economy was booming, and IT people were in huge demand, almost to the point that if one knew the basics about computers, he or she could be hired to be a programmer or database administrator, or for any other IT position.

At the end of 1997, a small company from New York City, operated by young Russian immigrants, arrived in Buffalo, New York. They promised to teach people how to write computer code in two months and be a reference for them when they looked for jobs. The company charged $4,000 for these services. The news spread quickly among the members of our Russian immigrant community in Buffalo. I concluded I was going to give it a chance. My girlfriend Tanya, and my cousin Rimma's husband, Yury, attended this course, too. For me, the subject was absolutely foreign—I had just recently become a computer user, but I knew nothing about computer code, networking, computer languages, and so on. I tried very hard to learn, as I thought it might be an opportunity for me to get a job in Information Technology.

Two months passed quickly, and I got familiar with some basic computer terminology and concepts, but, of course, I still did not have a deep knowledge of the subject. Nevertheless, I started to hunt for a position as a computer programmer in Buffalo. All of the Russian people who attended this course with me did the same. Buffalo is not a very big city, and even at the time of the dot-com bubble, job openings were scarce. Our resumes, prepared by the Russian company that gave us the course, were identical; only the names were different. According to these resumes, we all worked for the Russian company in New York City as programmers or database administrators, which, of course, was not true. Add to that how all of us were applying for the same open positions with the same companies in Buffalo. I remember that during one of my interviews, the person who was interviewing me asked me all kinds of questions—he was suspicious why suddenly so many Russian immigrants had applied for this job and all of them had the same credentials and had previously worked for the same company. His suspicions made me worried, and I realized I might need to move out of Buffalo in order to find a computer job and avoid being discovered as being involved in something not really legal.

Chapter Nineteen
Washington, D.C.

It was the spring of 1998. I still hoped to land a job in the IT industry. My friend, Lenny, had just moved to the Washington, D.C. area, and she said to me, "Come over. You might find a job here. You can stay with me while looking for a job." First, it felt like an impossible task: leave everything that was familiar in Buffalo and move to the unknown again. But events in my personal life propelled me to make a quick decision. I started the preparations for moving and also started a job hunt around the Washington, D.C. area, sending out my resume for jobs advertised in the newspapers or online. There were plenty of jobs around the Washington, D.C., Virginia, and Maryland corridor. I even got some feedback. One day, when I was ready, I hopped into my Toyota Corolla and drove to Washington, D.C. It was the first time I had to drive alone for such a long distance—around 400 miles. Smartphones with navigation systems were not yet known. I used a map, but I still got lost a few times. It was stressful, but I made it. Lenny was kind enough to give me one bedroom with a bathroom in her two-bedroom, two-bath apartment in the northwest part of the city. While I was looking for a computer programmer job, I got a job in a department store, where the hours were flexible, and it gave me the possibility to make some money.

After two months of job hunting and countless interviews, I got three job offers. I accepted the offer for the position of computer programmer/analyst from a company in Maryland. It was called "The Emmes Corporation". Emmes is a Hebrew word; it means truth. Emmes Corporation was (and still is) a company that provides clinical research and biostatistical services, infrastructure, and professional support for successful clinical research around the world. When I was hired in the summer of 1998, it was a small company with fewer than 100 employees. When I retired from this company seventeen-and-a-half years later, it was a mid-size company with around 800 employees.

I rented my own apartment as soon as I started my new job. It was a brand new one-bedroom in the Rio Center in Gaithersburg, Maryland, a very nice area with a man-made lake to walk around, a shopping area, and restaurants. It didn't hurt that it was in close proximity to my workplace. I was so happy to have a place to call home again.

I moved to my apartment from Lenny's on a Saturday and got busy unpacking and arranging my things there. I parked my car in a designated parking space in the parking lot. Even though I was given a parking permit hang tag, I was so busy that I forgot to hang it in my car. Around midnight I heard some strange noise in the parking lot—my apartment was on the first floor of the building. I remember thinking to myself, "What is going on in there?" A few minutes later, I looked out of my window and to my surprise did not see my car where I had left it in the parking lot. I thought, "So many years I lived in

Buffalo and this never happened to me. The first night I spent in Maryland, my car disappeared."

In distress, I went outside, hoping maybe someone had seen what had happened with my car. There was a woman outside, and I asked her if she had seen my car. She told me that one car had just been towed away because it had a New York license plate and no parking permit tag. I immediately realized that it must have been my car being towed and that was the noise I'd heard. They were pretty strict with violations there because across from our apartment building was a movie theater and people tried to use our parking spaces while going to watch a movie. The woman was kind enough to give me the phone of the car towing company. Early in the morning I called there and frantically tried to explain to the guy who picked up the phone that I just moved here, that I lived in the apartment, and that I really needed my car back. In response I heard, "Ma'am, you can come and pick up your car if you pay $700." So I did. It was a very traumatic prelude to my new beginning—in all my years in the United States, I had never had a driving ticket or had my car towed away from me before.

Chapter Twenty
Emmes

The first week I had a job orientation period during which my boss, Stuart, explained the nature of my work to me. But then the time came for me to write programs to make our applications work the way we wanted them to work—to collect and save data, do calculations behind the scenes, and many other tasks. I did not know where to start, as I did not have a sufficient knowledge base. When I was at my apartment after work, I could not stop thinking about my work and how I could learn before they kicked me out. I had a feeling that I was falling off a cliff. I needed help. I needed somebody who could teach me. I knew that before they hired me, a Russian-speaking programmer had worked at the position. I decided to find him and ask for help. So I did.

Alex started working with me on the weekends, and I paid him $25 per hour. We continued this collaboration for a month or so, and it was very helpful for me. In a few years, Alex returned to Emmes and eventually became Director of Software Development in the Computer Department. But then he suddenly got fired after many years of working there—he had some disagreement with the owner of the company.

My retirement in January 2016 from Emmes was

announced by the president and CEO of The Emmes Corporation on our internal website:

Author: Anne L.
Submitted: 01/12/2016 8:10:07 AM
After 18 years with Emmes, Larisa Gelya has announced she is retiring. Her final day at work with us will be Thursday, January 14, 2016.
Larisa joined Emmes while the company was still small enough to be located on the second floor of the Cabin John Mall, in June 1998, and to have our company meeting at Umberto's Italian Restaurant, which was also in the mall. Larisa grew up in Ukraine and worked in Uzbekistan before immigrating to the United States. We were fortunate that she chose Emmes!
Larisa is known for her openness and energy. Anyone who has visited her photo blogs can see she likes to share her life and the things she enjoys with others. Outside of work, she spends her time decorating her two homes, visiting local attractions, spending time with family, and traveling. A lot of traveling.
Here at Emmes, Larisa's attention to detail, commitment to our system's users, and testing skills are legendary. She would always strive to make any system she worked on error-free. When an error was discovered, Larisa would take the responsibility to ensure it was corrected rapidly.
Consequently, she was instrumental in making a number of Emmes IT initiatives successful. Among those were our first Java-based versions of AdvantageEDC, both our previous and current

versions of Web Form Builder, Offline Data Entry, TreatVars, Enrollment, and Global Trace. TreatVars and Enrollment, especially, would not be where they are today had it not been for Larisa's testing skills and commitment to excellence.

Like all our DRI's (DRI stands for Designated Responsible Individual—LG), while moving Emmes IT systems forward, Larisa also gave direct support to projects—at times as many as seven projects simultaneously. During her entire time with Emmes, Larisa has contributed to more than 30 projects. Along the way, she became our IT expert for our HIV studies. In fact, she has supported several Emmes HIV studies since their inception, including The International AIDS Vaccine Initiative (IAVI), HIV Brain Bank (HBB), HIV Solid Organ Transplant (HTR) and Rockefeller University's HIV studies (ROCK).

Larisa and her husband will be relocating to western Florida in the near future. We hope Larisa will look us up when she's in the area.

Thank you for all your contributions to Emmes, Larisa, and all the best in your well-deserved retirement!

I responded on the Intranet with my Emmes farewell letter:

Dear Colleagues,
January 14th is my last day at Emmes and on January 15th I'm starting a new chapter of my life—retirement years.

I worked at Emmes for 17.5 years and have indeed been incredibly fortunate to have been surrounded by many friends, mentors, respected business people, leaders and pioneers—all of you are special in your respective and unique ways.
I have been exposed to so many opportunities for my professional, as well as personal, growth. Challenges were set before me, advice was freely given, a helping hand extended.
May I extend my warmest thanks to everyone for the positive role that you have played in my life and my time at Emmes.
Well, they say that the downside of retirement is having to drink coffee on your own time. I am looking forward to a little more of my own time, but I will surely miss you all during my coffee breaks in the future.
Keep Emmes a success, stay well, and keep smiling.
Larisa Gelya, DRI/Programmer/Analyst

On January 14th, I emailed a "Goodbye" note to my IT group:

My Dear Colleagues—IT Group!
Thank you very much for showering me with your attention, the wonderful "Goodbye" lunch party, the card with warm wishes, generous gift, and photo album with memories about Emmes I'm looking forward to looking through!
You are a great group and I'll miss all of you!
Over seventeen and a half years with Emmes I have been knowing and working with some of you

for a long time and we became friends and comrades—developed a feeling of trust, a bond created by a shared goal and experience. I was privileged to learn from many of you and you have added a valuable dimension to my life. Thank you!

Twenty-six years ago I arrived in this country as a refugee without knowing any English. All my possessions were two suitcases mainly filled with family pictures and no penny in my pocket. I did not know how to start my life all over again in a new land. But this land was a land of opportunities! I learned that if you have the determination and work hard, you can reach your dreams!

And today I'm grateful to be able to move to the next chapter of my life! Please keep reaching for your dreams!

I'm wishing you all the best!

Larisa Gelya, DRI/Programmer/Analyst

For some reason, this last note touched the people in our IT department deeply. Perhaps many of them did not realize that I came to America with nothing and built my life from ground zero again. I do not know what it is, but many of my colleagues stopped by my office with tears in their eyes.

So, the beginning of the year 2016 became the end of my working years. It was also the end of seventeen years of driving every day for forty-two miles on the famous Beltway to get to work and back home. A new chapter of my life was about to start.

At work in the office at Emmes, Rockville, Maryland, 2016.

Chapter Twenty-One
Sparky

In the summer of 1999, I was pretty much settled in my cozy apartment in Gaithersburg, Maryland, and I loved living there. It had been one year since I had started to work at Emmes. I was busy at work but when I returned home after work, I felt lonely. I wanted to have someone special in my life, someone to love who would love me back, someone with whom I could share my life. One evening I was browsing the Internet, and I stumbled across a dating website. A very sincere ad caught my attention, and I replied to it. For one week it was back-and-forth email communication before we finally met face-to-face at the "Hamburger Hamlet" restaurant at Rio Center in Maryland on July 17, 1999. Sparky came with flowers, and it melted my heart. Since that day, we have never been apart.

When Sparky published his ad on the dating website, he had been a widower for three years. His wife of twenty years, Liz, had passed away from breast cancer. He had three sons: Andrew (from a first marriage), Matt, and Dan.

Sparky's official name is Emerson C. Norton, Jr. The nickname "Sparky" he got before he was born in 1949. His father was around fifty years old when his mother, thirty-five years old, became pregnant with their first child. Their friends started making jokes, telling his father, "Oh, you still have sparks in your blood!" When the baby was born, everyone in the family called him "Sparky". Six years later, Sparky's sister, Luciel, was born, but she had no nickname. Sparky's father, Emerson Norton, competed in the decathlon for the United States in the 1924 Summer Olympics, held in Paris, France. He won the silver medal. He is listed under "Emerson Norton" on Wikipedia.

Sparky lived in a house in Fairfax County, Virginia. It was a three-level house with a back patio and a big back yard. His youngest son, Dan, lived with Sparky at that time. When Sparky brought me for the first time to his house, I saw a not cozy and not well-kept house of a lonely man. Sparky said, "I know some things need to be done in the house, but I was not sure what to do." I always liked to make my home a cozy place, even when I lived in a tent in the geological expedition. Cozy means a lot of things—something that is comfy, lived in, warm, relaxing, happy, has good vibes, and is a place where one wants to hang out and relax. I wanted this house to be such a place.

So, a few days later, I asked Sparky, "Do you really want to do some improvements in your house?" When he said yes, the next week I arranged to meet with a Russian guy, Eugine, who had a business of remodeling houses. Eugine had been an architect in St. Petersburg in Russia before he immigrated to the United States. He came to the house to see it and make estimates for the project. Before long, Eugine and his team began remodeling Sparky's entire house; the project took seven months. While remodeling was going on, Sparky and I lived in my apartment in Maryland. It was fun coming to Virginia every weekend to see the progress and transformation of the house. In the end, we had a master suite with a large bathroom with a jacuzzi, guest bedroom, office, living room with a fireplace, family room, kitchen with brand new cabinets and granite countertops, and two more bathrooms. The freshly painted walls sparkled with cleanliness, and the light wooden floor was shiny. The fire burned brightly beneath the mantel in the living room. Our master bathroom with a huge jacuzzi and shower, with tiles covering the floor and reaching the ceiling, with mirrors that took up most of the walls above the vanity and jacuzzi, was the best piece of Eugine's creation. I decorated the house with beautiful wall pictures and other artifacts. Sparky and I bought new furniture. The house was transformed into a very warm and cozy place—the way I wanted it to be. We soon moved from my apartment in Maryland to the Virginia house.

Our Master bathroom in our house in Virginia.

Our Living room in our house in Virginia.

While the remodeling of the house in Virginia was in its last stages, my cousin Rimma's husband, Yury, moved in with us from Buffalo. As I mentioned before, he was attending the same computer course in Buffalo that I had, and, of course, he could not find a job in Buffalo upon completion of the course. My success with getting a job in Maryland encouraged him, especially since I had kept it for a year. So he came with the hope of finding a job in Washington, D.C., Virginia, or Maryland. He stayed with us for one and a half months. It was hard—Sparky and I had just started our life together, remodeling was still going on, and to have someone else in the house added extra stress. But Yury was part of the family and we wanted to help, even at the cost of our own convenience.

My cousin Rimma never fully appreciated our willingness to help them when they needed it—I found out about it much later, in 2013, when crazy things were happening in the family. Fortunately, Yury got a job, but the start period was so stressful for him that he suffered a heart attack and went through certain procedures in the hospital. The entire family moved from Buffalo to Virginia after he got out of the hospital. Yury is still working as a computer programmer even today. He and Rimma live and work in Virginia.

In May 2000, just before my birthday on May 12, we received a letter from Galina, Nikolai's girlfriend, from Poltava, Ukraine, that Nikolai Gelya, my first husband and father of my daughter, had gotten drunk and stepped out of a window of their sixth-floor apartment, saying, "I'm leaving." His daughter Anna, whom he'd had with my former girlfriend, Olga, had been visiting him at the time. This news was shocking to us. A little later, we sent money to Anna so she could buy a decent gravestone for Nikolai. We do not know if she did. I corresponded with Galina for some time and even sent her money when she had surgery, but then her letters stopped coming. All I know is that she had a married son with two children, whom she visited often. For Natasha and me, it was difficult to take in how Nikolai ended his life. We were deeply and utterly bewildered and sad, having never expected what had occurred.

Life is like a game of chess. To win, you have to make a move. But sometimes even to live is an act of courage.

In the summer of 2000, we bought a miniature white poodle. He was born on June 6, 2000; when we brought him to the Virginia home, he was eight weeks old and was the size of my palm. We named him Sasha. Sasha was a beloved member of our family for seventeen years and four months. He loved to run in our back yard and walk in the park with Sparky. Sasha traveled with us a lot—by car and by airplane. We groomed Sasha by ourselves. He was a very sweet and beloved dog. He passed away on October 7, 2017, in Florida.

That same year, 2000, my cousin Vitalik immigrated from Yalta, Ukraine. He came by himself; his parents stayed in Yalta. Originally, Vitalik lived with Rimma and Yury—they had just bought a house in Virginia. I invited Vitalik to move into our house because I thought we had better living conditions for him and could provide better help with finding his way in a new country. Back in Yalta, Vitalik had been working as a doctor. We knew that becoming a doctor in the United States would require a lot of hard work and would take a long time. Vitalik stayed with us for one-and-a-half years until he could get a decent job and rent his own apartment. Today Vitalik works as a doctor at the Cleveland Clinic and lives in Cleveland, Ohio, with his wife, Ella, and son, Erik.

Vitalik, Ella and Erik, Virginia, 2014.

Sparky and I got married on October 14, 2000, in our back yard. It was a warm and tender autumn day. Our back yard was nicely decorated with a wedding arch and flowers. All of our children and relatives came to celebrate with us. We exchanged vows: "I take you to be my wife/husband, to have and to hold from this day forward, for better, for worse, for richer, for poorer, in sickness and in health, to love and to cherish, till death us do part, and this is my solemn vow."

Our wedding on October 14, 2000 - with our children.

On September 18, 2003, Hurricane Isabel hit Virginia. The entire night Isabel raged outside the window, I heard the wind howl, and our large trees groaned in our backyard under the weight of the huge monstrosity of the wind and heavy rain. I was petrified. I could not sleep, so I just stared at the ceiling and wondered if we would survive. With the first morning light, I looked out of the window from our second-floor bedroom and saw a huge old tree with roots up in our back yard. We were lucky—the tree fell on the fence opposite the house. We had to pay $4,000 to remove the fallen tree from the yard, but later our home insurance returned this money to us. A large hole was left in the middle of our back yard; we were not sure what to do about it.

The fallen tree in our back yard after hurricane Isabel, 2003.

One day we went to see the "Home and Garden" show, and there I got an idea about building a pond with a waterfall, koi fish, and a flower bed around it. Sparky did not want it at first, but he finally succumbed to the idea. We hired people to do the work. They started in the morning when we went to work. When we came back from work, there was a pond with a waterfall instead of a big hole. The sound of running water was incredibly soothing. I planted flowers around the area, and we bought koi fish. Soon our pond became a central attraction of our back yard, and it was beautiful. Everyone admired it! So many gatherings and celebrations with family and friends took place in our back yard. I hope my grandchildren will always remember our back yard in Virginia—they spent so many happy times there.

Our dog Sasha and our Pond in Virginia.

Our Pond in Virginia.

Flowers in our back yard in Virginia.

Water lily in our Pond, Virginia.

Water lily in our Pond, Virginia.

We had a very special relationship with the parents of Liz, Sparky's wife, who passed away—Grandma and Grandpa Opyd. When they still had their house in Chicago, they traveled from their farmhouse in North Carolina to Chicago (and back) by car. They always stopped for the night at our house in Virginia during their travels. When we went on vacations, they babysat our dog Sasha in our house. When they sold their house in Chicago and moved to the farmhouse in North Carolina permanently, we visited them there quite often. I was so grateful to them for accepting me as their daughter and showering me with love and kindness, always ready to help. In June 2015, they celebrated seventy years together. We celebrated with them. They passed away soon after that: Martin Opyd passed away on December 22, 2015, and Elizabeth Opyd passed away on May 6, 2017. There was a memorial service on July 29, 2017, in North Carolina, near the farm where they spent so many years of their lives. Sparky and I, as well as all other family members, attended this service. Their kindness, inspiration, unconditional love, and support made our lives so much brighter. I think about them often.

Those we love can never be more than a thought apart. For as long as there is a memory, they'll live on in our hearts.

Martin and Elizabeth Opyd, North Carolina, June 2015.

We sold our Virginia house in the spring of 2016. It was on the market for only three days. Sparky had lived there for thirty-eight years, and I for seventeen. We felt sad preparing it for sale.

A young couple bought the house. They did remodeling to open up the kitchen and made it into one great area with a living room. They told us that in the spring we left, the three koi fish in the pond had babies, about 200 of them. Tricia and Kivins, the new owners of the house, were overwhelmed and not sure what to do with all of the babies, so they gave them away. We were quite surprised because in all the years when we had koi fish in the pond, we never had babies. Later on, when Tricia and Kivins had their first child, a baby girl, they got rid of the pond in the back yard.

Family gathering on our back porch in Virginia.

Chapter Twenty-Two
9/11

September 11, 2001, appeared no different from any other late summer day in the big, metropolitan D.C. area. I was driving to work on the Capital Beltway from Virginia to Maryland when National Public Radio (NPR) announced that a plane had flown into one of the twin towers of the World Trade Center in New York City. After this announcement, NPR continued its normally scheduled program. My brain could not process what I had just heard, and I became nervous. Had I understood correctly? A plane flew into the twin towers? How? Why? I wanted to get to my destination as soon as possible, get on the Internet, and find out what happened. When I arrived at Emmes, I saw people gathered in small groups near computer screens. I joined a group of people from our department. We stared at the screen in disbelief, watching the events unfolding in New York City, the report of the first plane crashing into the North Tower, and then the second going into the South Tower. It was then we understood it was a terrorist attack. Shortly after the report, Emmes let all employees go home for the rest of the day.

In distress, I drove back home on the already congested beltway. I thought we might be at war. For the rest of the day, we watched TV at home. As if in a horror movie, we watched the twin towers crumbled, diminished to dust. The structural steel of the skyscrapers, built to withstand winds over 200 miles per hour and a large conventional fire, could not withstand the tremendous heat generated by the burning jet fuel. We learned that nineteen terrorists had hijacked four airplanes. They carried out suicide attacks against different targets in the United States. These terrorists were associated with the Islamic extremist group, Al-Qaeda. In New York City, two planes hit the World Trade Center twin towers, a third plane hit the Pentagon just outside of Washington, D.C., a thirty-minute drive from our home, and a fourth plane crashed in a field in Pennsylvania, near Shanksville. The last of these flights, United 93, was hijacked about forty minutes after leaving Newark Liberty International Airport in New Jersey. Because the plane had been delayed in taking off, passengers on board learned of the events in New York and Washington via cell phones. The passengers fought the four hijackers. There is a belief that they attacked the cockpit with a fire extinguisher. The plane then flipped over and sped toward the ground, crashing in a rural field near Shanksville in western Pennsylvania at 10:10 a.m. All forty-four people aboard were killed. The intended targets of hijackers are not known, but theories include the White House, the U.S. Capitol, the Camp David presidential retreat in Maryland, or one of several nuclear power plants along the eastern seaboard.

More than 3,000 people never made it home that night. We witnessed the largest terrorist attack on American soil since the attack on Pearl Harbor in 1941. Many weeks passed before I was able to fully process the events of that day. Our innocence on our home front was forever shattered. From that point, we have looked at the world and ourselves differently.

Eighteen years later, in October of 2019, Sparky and I traveled to New York City. We visited the "National September 11 Memorial Museum" that was built where the World Trade Center twin towers once proudly stood. The somber memory of September 11, 2001, will stay with me forever.

Twin Towers in NYC on September 11, 2001.

Chapter Twenty-Three
Grandchildren

"Your children are your rainbows and your grandchildren are your pot of gold."
–Unknown

It is an honor to become a grandparent. Grandchildren connect the lines from generation to generation and make life complete.

On November 11, 2001, in Buffalo, New York, our first grandson, Kyle Greene, came into this world. Sparky, our dog Sasha, and I had driven to Buffalo from Virginia. On November 11, we went to the hospital to meet Kyle for the first time. There are not enough words to express the feeling I had when we saw Kyle through the hallway window in the hospital nursery. My heart was melting from the overwhelming joy—he was a continuation of my life. When I'm gone, he will continue to carry on the torch of life and pass it to future generations along with little pieces of my soul. We loved him from the first second we saw him, and we watched him in fascination. From the first glance, it was quite clear that Kyle resembles Brian more than Natasha.

Our second grandson, Connor Greene, arrived in this world on April 8, 2003, also in Buffalo. We came from Virginia after he was born, and again my heart melted from joy. Holding Connor in our hands was mesmerizing. We saw right away that Connor resembled

Natasha more than Brian. His big brown eyes always looked at the world with wonder and curiosity.

We drove to Buffalo for holidays and on every occasion when we could take time off from work—we wanted to see our grandchildren as much as we could. It always amazed us that for daily walks Natasha took the boys to the Buffalo Zoo. From an early age, they already knew most of the animals in the zoo. What made me upset, though, was the fact that Natasha and Brian decided to take a novel approach with Connor and teach him to be more independent—at night they just put him in his crib and let him cry until he fell asleep. When I was there, I could not stand his crying. I would stay with him and sing a lullaby for him until he fell asleep.

Our grandsons Connor (left) and Kyle, first Christmas in Virginia, 2005.

In August 2005, Natasha, Brian, Kyle, and Connor moved to Virginia from Buffalo. Brian got a job in the Institute for Defense Analyses (IDA) in Alexandria, just outside of Washington, D.C. They lived with us in our Falls Church house for two months until they bought their own house in Burke, Virginia. We celebrated Kyle's fourth birthday in our backyard. An inflatable moon bounce house was installed, and many guests were invited to celebrate with us.

Inflatable moon bounce house installed in our back yard in Virginia, 2005.

For many years, Connor and Kyle came to our house on Friday mornings to stay over the weekend. For that reason, I stopped working on Fridays and worked only four days a week. Sparky installed a big playground in our back yard, filled with swing sets and slides, and jungle gyms. We played, read books, did projects, and watched movies. Going with Sparky and Sasha for a morning walk, playing The Lego Game, spending time on the playground, and chasing Sasha around the house were their favorite activities.

Connor, Kyle, Sparky and our dog Sasha in our back yard, Virginia, 2005.

Connor (left) Sparky and Kyle in our home in Virginia, 2007.

Our third grandson, Enzo Norton-Mitchell, Sparky's son Andrew's child, was born on June 21, 2004, in Lawrence, Kansas. The first time we met him was when he was a few months old. Handsome and sweet, with big blue eyes and curly hair, Enzo loved to play with his two big dogs and Thomas the Train. Enzo and his parents live in Texas now. They visit us in Florida when they can, and it is the happiest time for us when we are all together.

Our Grandson Enzo, Kansas, 2006.

Our fourth grandson, long waited for, Henry Norton, Sparky's son Matt's child, was born on February 1, 2018, in Fairfax, Virginia. Henry is a warm, good-natured little guy with amazing blue eyes that look directly into your soul and try to figure you out. We communicate with him via "FaceTime" almost every week and are looking forward to his visits at Christmas time.

Our Grandson Henry, SW Florida, 2021.

Chapter Twenty-Four
North Port

We went to North Port in Southwest Florida for the very first time in the summer of 2007. I had heard from my girlfriend Tanya from Buffalo about the Warm Mineral Springs in the area; she went there for vacation and liked it. We decided to check it out. We rented a house near the Springs and spent a week there. It was a good time—our days were consumed by the Warm Mineral Springs, and in the late afternoon we drove to Manasota Beach. The only thing that was strange was that most visitors at the Warm Mineral Springs were Russian or Polish immigrants. Many lived around the Warm Mineral Springs. Also, many Russians vacationed there from other states. Sparky said, "For the first time I feel like a foreigner in my own country." Nowadays, a lot of Americans can be seen spending a relaxing day at Warm Mineral Springs—they finally came to appreciate this Florida gem, too. Vacation rentals were and still are a very popular business there.

Warm Mineral Springs, North Port, SW Florida.

Warm Mineral Springs are naturally formed mineral springs. Its temperature is a consistent 85-87 degrees year-round. The water is low in oxygen (anaerobic). There is a belief that water has been trapped underground for over 30,000 years at depths over 7,000 feet. Under this depth and pressure, the water is geothermally heated to 97 degrees Fahrenheit. When it reaches the surface, the temperature drops to between 85 and 87 degrees Fahrenheit. The underwater survey states that eight million gallons of water a day are running the natural way on the surface and eventually into the Gulf of Mexico.

Warm Mineral Springs' water has the highest mineral content in America and ranks as the third-highest mineral content in the world. There are over fifty-one different minerals found in the rich water at Warm Mineral Springs, each one offering its own unique health benefits that are absorbed naturally through the skin, helping to remineralize one's body and promote health and healing.

Chemical analysis of the water reveals that Warm Mineral Springs' water is comparable to the mineral contents of the waters of such famed international spas as Vichy and Aix Les Bains in France, Hot Springs in Arkansas, and Baden Baden in Germany. The Warm Mineral Springs' mineral density results in high buoyancy for bathers, which helps to sustain effortless swimming and the joy of weight-free movement. The only drawback is that the water smells like sulfur because of the mineral content.

In the summer of 2008, we rented a big house in North Port and brought our grandchildren and children with us for vacation. Natasha came with Kyle and Connor, Enzo with his parents Andrew and Amy, and us. Unfortunately, Amy had to go back home to Kansas after two days due to unexpected job demands. We introduced them to Warm Mineral Springs and our favorite, Manasota Beach. Every time Enzo took a dip into the Warm Mineral Springs, he exclaimed, "Stinky water! Stinky water!" Enzo was five years old then, but his "Stinky water!" cry became our secret code for that vacation, and it stays in our memory forever. Even now, when we want to go to the Warm Mineral Springs for a day, one of us certainly will say, "Let's go to 'Stinky water!'" The house we rented during that visit included a swimming pool, so our grandkids had an entire week of bliss there.

Kyle, Connor and Enzo at Warm Mineral Springs in SW Florida, 2008.

Kyle at Venice Beach, SW Florida, 2008.

The Great Recession hit in 2008. It was caused by the 2007 financial crisis when the breakdown of trust between banks occurred. Deregulation permitted banks to employ hedge fund trading with derivatives. That caused the subprime mortgage crisis—interest-only loans became available to high-risk borrowers who were most likely to default. Low-interest rates were offered in the beginning. But these "too-good-to-be-true" loans were reset to a much higher rate after a certain period. At the same time, home prices fell. Many homeowners were trapped—they couldn't afford the payments, and they couldn't sell their homes. That created the financial crisis that led to the Great Recession.

In Florida, the Great Recession was much more pronounced than in Northern Virginia. People lost their jobs, and every second house was for sale. When the house sale was unsuccessful, the home was simply left to the bank, and all belongings were sold via garage sale for pennies. Developers left the area with unfinished business. Brand-new houses were sold in North Port at unbelievably low prices. With sadness, we observed the situation in Florida, but we had our jobs waiting for us at home in Virginia and felt secure, despite what we saw around us.

On the morning of our last vacation day in North Port, I said to Sparky, "Let's go see houses here that are for sale. Why are they so cheap?" And off we went. By the end of the day, we gave an offer on a three-bedroom, two-bath house at 4594 Appleton Terrace in North Port. The house was brand new and owned by the bank. The next morning we went back home to Virginia. All of the paperwork and transactions were done via the Internet. In less than one month we became the owners of our second house, our Florida house in North Port.

Our house in North Port, SW Florida, 2008.

Since we were still working, we decided to rent out our house in Florida as a vacation property for most of the year. Also, it would be available for our vacation and for family members and friends for free.

For the next few months in Virginia, I visited "second hand" stores, looking for items to furnish and decorate our Florida house. Then we took a ten-day vacation, packed Sparky's red truck, and drove to Florida. We had only one week to make our new, empty house livable and ready to be rented as a vacation property. Sparky and I worked from the morning to late evening, we visited many garage sales, we brought in furniture, we decorated the walls with pictures, and we equipped the kitchen. By the end of our vacation, the house felt warm and cozy. I even planted trees, bushes, and flowers around the house. It was ready to accept our first tenants. I launched what would become a successful eight-year vacation rental business. I managed all operations via the Internet. The cleaning of the house, after each tenant left, and a repair when needed, was done by the local Russian managers, husband and wife, whom we hired for that. I really enjoyed this little business.

Driving from Virginia to North Port, SW Florida, December 2008.

Natasha went for a Florida vacation with the boys just once, and they stayed in our house there. My cousin Bella from Chicago and her husband Emil stayed in our North Port house twice. Pasha, Alesya, and their children, Romik and Julia, from Cleveland, also stayed in our house. They are relatives of my cousin Vitalik's wife, Ella. My girlfriend Tanya from Buffalo stayed in our house while vacationing in Florida. Our friends from Austria, Zoya and her husband Walter, stayed with us there for a few days. We first met Zoya when she worked in NIH (National Institute of Health) in Maryland for one year. She was visiting us often in our Virginia house at that time. We went to our North Port house every year in

December before Christmas to take care of things, including doing deep cleaning, and getting it ready for the next vacation rental season. When we go to the Warm Mineral Springs now from Valencia Lakes, we try to drive by our old house on Appleton Terrace in North Port just to see how the new owners take care of the house. The house has a sentimental value to us and to see it well-kept gives us satisfaction.

Living Room in our North Port House, SW Florida, 2016.

Living Room in our current house, Valencia Lakes, SW Florida, 2021.

Chapter Twenty-Five
The Madness of the Year 2013

"Know your worth—you must find the courage to leave
the table if respect is no longer being served."
—Tene Edwards

It is difficult to write about events that happened which still elicit strong, painful emotions. Events that can still bring tears when trying to put words to paper. Reliving certain memories can carry a heavy emotional toll. But it is the examination by the person you are now, rather than the person you were then. Often the shedding of new tears can help you move forward and find the courage to write your story. Writing your story can give you a sense of closure and reduce your pain.

In the spring of 2013, my cousin Vova, with his family—wife Lili and three teenage children, Shay, Zahar, and Hen—relocated from Israel to the United States. They had been waiting for visas for about ten years since the time when my Aunt Inna filled out papers for the family reunification. The last time I saw Vova was in 1989, just before I left the Soviet Union; he was young and unmarried at that time. We had never seen Lili and their children before—we had only heard about them. We were very excited to meet all of them. We invited all of our relatives for dinner many times. Children played in our back yard, my grandchildren mingled with Vova's children, and we were glad that they met each other. I thought to myself, "How nice that five more people are added to our family. We all can be together now for the holidays and family events." But things soured rather quickly.

We all still lived in Virginia then. Vova's family stayed in his sister Rimma's house. The relocation from one country to another and the adaptation process are never easy tasks and always involve a lot of stress. People who choose this path in life need to possess a lot of strength and determination. In turn, people who accept them at their new destination need to exhibit a lot of patience and provide moral and financial support. This is not a simple task, and it exceeded the capabilities of my cousin Rimma. She could not prepare her house and herself for hosting five people. On top of this, my cousin Vova was always a strange man. My Aunt Inna, his mother, is amazingly capable of creating drama from a difficult family situation. She was like a "broken record," endlessly repeating the same words and phrases until one wants to scream and cry. In a flash, the atmosphere was set to unhealthy and toxic. Very soon, the tensions among all of them reached a quite uncomfortable level. Inna and Rimma decided that Vova, Lili, and their children should go back to Israel and stay there. However, Lili did not want to go back to Israel.

In addition to all of this, the stress and toxic environment caused Vova to develop some health problems with his GI system. He could not see a doctor since they did not have any medical insurance in the United States, but they still had their medical coverage in Israel. So Inna and Rimma pushed them to go back to Israel, creating a false story they told all around them:

"Vova is very ill, almost dying, and, could you imagine, that Lili, his wife, does not want to go back to Israel to take care of her husband?" They pressed Lili hard every day and started a devaluing campaign against her. I did not know Lili very well, but I observed that among all adults—Inna, Rimma, Vova—she was the most normal. She appeared to be a strong and determined woman in contrast to her husband. All she needed was moral support, a peaceful environment, and a roof above their heads just for a few months—all these things their relatives could not, and would not, provide for them. I tried to help as much as I could—I took Shay to Emmes with me for an interview in the hope he could, perhaps, get a summer job there; he had an interview but did not get a job. Later on, Shay got a job at Tysons Corner Mall selling Dead Sea cosmetics. The company also gave him a room in an apartment. When he was done with this job, he stayed in our house for a week.

Being under constant and great pressure, Lili, Vova, and Hen finally went back to Israel to take Vova to the doctor. Zahar stayed in Virginia with Rimma. Soon, the school year was about to start. Earlier, Rimma had signed up Zahar and Hen for the school to which they had to be driven—there were no buses available to take them to that school from Rimma's house. With everybody in Rimma's household working, who could drive the kids to and from school every day? When I asked Rimma this question, she just shrugged and said, "We will figure it out. I'm going to transfer Zahar to the school near me so he can take a bus." On the Internet, I found out that, according to Virginia law, only parents of a child can transfer the child from one school to another. I sent this information with a link to the website to Rimma, and to

Lili in Israel. Lili and Hen were about to return to Virginia before the school year started, but Rimma said that they could not stay in her house anymore. Inna and Rimma had a plan that Lili, Zahar, and Hen would stay in Inna's apartment. But there were two problems with that—Lili was not driving, and they could stay in Inna's apartment for only three weeks as guests according to apartment building rules. Vova was not planning to return to Virginia yet. I thought that the way Inna and Rimma treated Lili was pretty outrageous. I was very sympathetic to Lili and tried to help her. I arranged an interview for her with a company that trained people how to be testers for computer programs, and when Lili arrived, I took her for the interview.

My relatives united against me as soon as they understood I would not join them in opposing Lili, but after her interview, all hell broke loose. When Inna and Rimma smudged and tarnished my credibility and my character, and cast a negative light on my personhood, it devastated my spirit and feeling of self-worth. To my astonishment and horror, my daughter Natasha sided with them. She displayed no loyalty, no love to me; she did not attempt to understand me and my position in this situation. Her attitude was: "Are you against my mother? Great, I'm with you!" All three of them—Inna, Rimma, and my Natasha—talked nonsense about me behind my back, belittling me. I remember I had a feeling that I wanted to go to the moon to escape the hell of our family. The culmination of all of these events happened on October 4th when I went to Natasha's house to talk with her.

Our talk did not go very well, as Natasha exhibited only anger. She did not want to listen to what I wanted to say or what I felt. Then she did something I would never expect or imagine. She opened the door and yelled at me, "Mother, get out of my house or I will call the police!" Was it my daughter who just yelled these awful words at me? She usually called me "Mom," not "Mother". Police? What was she going to call the police for? It was more than shocking, I was shattered. I stood there, frozen, unsure of what to do. I felt paralyzed, cemented in place. It was more than I could bear. Not knowing how to react, I just said, "I cannot believe I gave you life and raised you!" I felt I could not breathe; I needed fresh air. I walked through the open door and left. I have not been in her house again since that time. I had post-traumatic stress disorder for many years, problems with sleeping at night, and I was ashamed (and still am). This happened on October 4th, 2013.

The same evening, Natasha called Sparky. She was crying and telling him she kicked me out of her house; she mentioned what I said to her, but she omitted to tell him she threatened me with the police. Sparky did not tell me about their phone conversation for a month—he was trying to protect me from being upset. At the same time, I did not tell him about what happened between Natasha and me for a month because I was so embarrassed. I could not tell what had happened to anyone! After one month I told Sparky what was going on and he told me about their phone conversation. Sparky and I came to the conclusion we needed to take the first step and talk with her. Natasha would not want to come to talk at our house, so we agreed to meet in the restaurant near her house (not the best place to have such a tough conversation). She insisted she wanted to bring my cousin Rimma with her (Rimma and my Aunt Inna remained Natasha's cheerleaders in this unfortunate situation, to my disbelief).

Our attempt to make peace did not go well. Natasha had the attitude of an angry teenager, even though she was 44 years old at the time. Instead of having any remorse, she said, "Do you know how easy it is for me to call the police? I just need to dial one number." I thought it was not my daughter, or she had some mental problem all of a sudden. I was at a loss. We left. I made many other attempts to talk with her, but every time I came across the same angry attitude of a teenager and brutality.

I arranged with a psychologist who was ready to work with both of us. After I had a session, the psychologist told me that now she would like to hear Natasha's perspective. I emailed Natasha and I said that I would pay for all of our appointments. Natasha refused to see her. Meanwhile, my relatives supported and cheered her on in her attitude towards me. She invited them to my grandchildren's birthday parties, and we, their grandparents, were not invited, and so on and on. It was something we were unable to comprehend. The stress, the pain, the shame—it was a real torture, and I could not stop asking myself, "Why?" Sparky wrote letters to her, but she never responded. I did not know what to do. I wanted to believe that she would remember all the love and care we had given her and her children, that she would understand how much we needed them and how much they needed us, that she would call to tell us how sorry she was, that she did not mean to hurt us. But weeks, months, years passed by and nothing changed. I thought that for some unknown reason she'd lost her heart; it had been replaced with a piece of ice, just like in the children's story, "The Snow Queen," written by Hans

Christian Andersen. It is a story about the struggle between good and evil—a bedtime story I told my grandchildren so many times.

One awful episode etched in my memory forever happened during the summer of 2015, when my cousin Serezha from Yalta, Crimea (that became part of Russia), and his wife Lena were visiting us in Virginia. They were staying in our house. One evening they were ready to go for dinner with the other part of our family—my Aunt Inna, my cousin Rimma, and perhaps, my daughter, Natasha. Sparky and I were not participating —we were on the other end of the broken family puzzle. I was sitting on the front porch, while Serezha and Lena were getting ready. The car came to our driveway. It was Natasha's car and she was driving. Rimma was sitting in the passenger seat. Rimma got out of the car and said, "Hello, Larisa." I said, "Hello, Rimma." Natasha stayed in the car, not one word from her. Serezha and Lena came out of the house and walked towards the car in the driveway. Natasha started the car. At this moment I heard Connor's voice inside the car, but I could not see him. I froze in place. They brought Connor and would not let him get out of the car to say "hello" to his grandparents?! Connor, who knew exactly where he was, Connor, who had been coming to our house every Friday to stay with us for the weekends, was ordered to stay inside the car and was not allowed to see his grandparents?! I was speechless! It was a manifestation of human brutality I had never experienced before! I went inside the house, curled up on the sofa, and moaned. I thought, "Who are these people? Was it my daughter? Was it my cousin? Do they understand what they are doing?" I felt a dark blanket of depression wrapping around me. I wanted to be on the moon again. Sparky silently sat by me, trying to comfort me with his presence. I do not believe that both of them, Natasha and Rimma, understood the cruelty they inflicted on us, and it is very sad. Rimma now has grandchildren of her own. I'm wondering how would she feel if I supported her daughter in the same kind of behavior?

On August 1, 2015, Elina, Rimma's daughter, was getting married. Everyone, including my daughter, was invited, except us. I would expect my daughter to protest and stand up for her mother and say something like, "If you do not invite my mother, I cannot attend either." I did this for my daughter before, and not just once. But Natasha took her children and her husband and enjoyed the wedding. Did my grandchildren ask why their grandparents were not invited? Probably not. To us, it was an act of betrayal and another addition to stress, disbelief, and sadness.

When we started to think about our retirement plans, I wanted us to move to another country—I felt I could not take what was going on in our family any longer. I did research on the Internet to find out which countries welcome American retirees. From what I learned, it appeared that Cuenca in Ecuador would be an easy and pleasant place to retire. I was not afraid to move there. But, of course, Sparky was frightened by my plans. He said, "I'll go with you where you want to go, but just remember that I do not want to live in another country." I knew that a change in the country and learning a new language would be difficult for both of us, but he would suffer the most. So, I needed to change my thinking.

In 2016, we moved to Florida. We went back to Virginia a few times to visit our (Sparky's) son and a newborn grandson. I wrote to Natasha in advance, saying that we would like to see our grandchildren and, perhaps, her too, but every time she said "No". I felt terrified. It made me literally ill. I have not seen my grandchildren for eight years now. I had not even seen any pictures of them until last year, when my sister from Belarus sent me one that my Aunt Inna sent to her. There seemed to be nothing I could change, and I could not take such abuse anymore. I concluded that since I could not change the situation, I needed to change my attitude to it. I refused to accept this emotional chaos as normal. I needed to gain a much-desired sense of emotional balance. It was hard to achieve and still is. I finally realized that what happened between Natasha and me has a name—parents being abused by their adult children. Abuse crosses all social, cultural, and economic lines—poor and rich, educated and not. Parents who are abused have one thing in common—despair. Perhaps the biggest obstacles to overcoming parent abuse are shame and blame. As with any form of abuse, the people being hurt must recognize that they are not at fault and do not deserve it.

During our life in Zarafshan, Uzbekistan, even when life was especially tough and felt unbearable, I comforted myself with a thought: "As long as my child is healthy and okay, we can get through this. Nothing else really matters." My child was the most important thing to me. When and how did I miss noticing my daughter turning into a person I do not want her to be? I failed Natasha somewhere along the way, and I'm very sorry about it.

Happily, I can communicate with my grandchildren via phone messages. When they were smaller, they rarely replied, but I kept writing and sending pictures and videos to them. When we were still working, we put aside money for Kyle and Connor to help with their college educations. Kyle's first year in college was 2020, and I paid his tuition for both the fall and spring semesters. We never missed a birthday or holiday season—I always showered my grandsons with gifts, cards, and other expressions of love. Now that they are nineteen and eighteen, they do reply to my messages more often. I can imagine that they are confused and sense the awkwardness of the situation in our family—their mother and grandmother not talking for many years. What can I do? I'm trying to do what is right for my situation.

It is during our darkest moments that we must focus to see the light.

All my adult years, I have worked so hard to reach toward love and safety. The saddest irony of life is that after everything I went through to get to the United States and bring my daughter here, I lost her. Somehow life finds a way of throwing challenges at us.

Recently, I found on the Internet this explanation of grief by Jamie Anderson:

Grief, I've learned, is really just love. It's all the love you want to give, but cannot. All that unspent love gathers up in the corners of your eyes, in the lump in your throat, and in that hollow part of your chest. Grief is just love with no place to go.

This explanation resonates with me. I went through all five stages of grief—denial, anger, bargaining, depression, and acceptance. I feel that grief inhabited my body and is still dwelling there.

When Lili returned to Virginia from Israel in August 2013 and assessed the situation, she was smart enough to escape the hell that Inna and Rimma created. She bought tickets to California. She had an old girlfriend there who gave her and her children a room in her house and the moral support they needed so much. After a few months, Lili with children rented their own apartment. Lili got a job as a piano teacher, and her children went to school. Shay, the oldest boy, went back to Israel to attend a medical college. Now he is working and living in Israel. Vova came to California later. He never worked there and is still not working now. They still live together, but I heard Vova is planning to return to Israel with their daughter, Hen, after she graduates from school in June 2021. Zahar, their son, already finished college and got a job, so Lili and Zahar are going to stay in California.

Family is supposed to be our safe haven. Very often, it's the place where we find the deepest heartache.

Lili (left), Shay and Hen, Virginia, 2013.

Zahar (left) and Shay, Virginia, 2013.

Chapter Twenty-Six
The Precious Gifts of Life

Just when it feels like everything has been lost, life brings surprises with its precious gifts, like it wants to provide assurance that the world is big and life is so full of unpredictable beauty and inexplicable wonders.

In November 2014, I met (via the Internet) my dear friend Valya, my kindred spirit. She is the daughter of my friend Lydia from the time before I left the Soviet Union, who lives in Russia now. Valya wanted to improve her English language skills by communicating in English, and I agreed to help her. We started to communicate, and very soon I discovered a beautiful soul, a curious mind, a powerful spirit, a great imagination. Our interaction is ongoing and gives me a feeling of great connections of our souls and spirits, something not easily found in this world. Since the time we first met, Valya has become an English teacher and advanced her career to a management position in the college. Here is an excerpt from her latest email to me:

> *It is always such a pleasure to get your emails! I read them at once and then reread and think how lucky I am. There are so many people all around, but hardly ever is there somebody who understands you and can talk to you about everything. I found you, my dear friend, on the other side of our planet and can't stop needing*

you in my life. Thank you, Lara! You are an amazing person. My achievements for these seven years mostly belong to you. Really. I learn your stories, see your photos with you smiling in them—and that gives me a great power for going on. I want you to be happy, you are very important to me...

When I read these words, I could not hold my tears back. I thought about my daughter; I wanted to hear those words from her! I wanted to have Valya as my daughter! She is a splendid gift in my life.

My Friend Valya, Russia, 2021.

I developed strong bonds with my favorite niece Oksana and her little boy, Nik. Oksana became like a daughter to me, and Nik calls me "grandma". They live in Belarus, but we talk via Skype very often. Every year I send them packages with wonderful things from America. It makes me happy when they can enjoy my gifts.

My niece Oksana, Gomel, 2019.

Oksana's son, Nik, Gomel, 2020.

And of course, I'm so lucky to have my husband Sparky—he stood by me when I felt that I was "losing the ground beneath my feet," when I felt I would rather be on the moon.

My husband Sparky, Valencia Lakes, SW Florida, 2021.

When our beloved dog, Sasha, passed away in October 2017, we mourned him for a long time—he was a family member for more than seventeen years. Then, after one year passed, we decided to get a new puppy. Charlie, a black miniature poodle, came into our lives in the fall of 2018 when he was nine weeks old. His personality differs greatly from Sasha's—Sasha was a sweet dog who liked to cuddle, to always be close to us, and to show his love and affection to us. Charlie, in contrast, is "Mister Independent," but he likes to play games and be trained to do different tricks. He makes our life so enthralling. For us, Charlie is a precious gift of life, too.

Charlie, Valencia Lakes, SW Florida, 2021.

Since we retired and moved to Valencia Lakes—55+ Active Adults Community in southwest Florida—our life, before the COVID-19 pandemic started, was very interesting; we traveled to faraway and fascinating countries and amazing places near us; our travels painted our life in dazzling colors. When we traveled, we made a lot of pictures and video clips and I always wrote my travel notes about places we visited. Upon returning home, I was busy editing my pictures and notes, then creating videos I published on YouTube. These activities have always given me a sense of fulfillment and purpose in life—the knowledge that something will be left of me after I'm gone. I started my video creation a long time ago—my first video was a gift for Sparky's 60th birthday and an attempt to tell a picture story of his life from his earlier years to the day when he turned sixty years old. Since that time, I have created a video for every family event and every trip we have taken. I have a channel on

YouTube—Lgelya. It is still my favorite pastime activity.

Once upon a time, already being here in the United States, I Googled my name, and to my amusement, I found an article about Zarafshan and about me, actually regarding my video that I created in February 2011 about our life in the Kyzylkum Desert.

The article was named "In Zarafshan" and written on October 27, 2011, by Tyler Olsen. He incorrectly stated that I lived in North Dakota—at the time I was in Northern Virginia. Olsen wrote about Googling Zarafshan:

> *Cruising and boozing around Uzbekistan, a Canadian reporter winds up in a place that gives no logical reason to visit, where the question Why? has no answer. Fortunately, virtual travel remains risk-free, except for all the beer.*
>
> *The orange sand slides away beneath me as I meander down a long boulevard, the harsh sun stabbing at me from behind the trees. The ground soon turns to pavement as I cross four lanes of deserted, unused roadway and find myself alone in the middle of a massive, barren public square. Is this place abandoned or, markedly worse, inhabited by zombies? I think, as I walk to the fridge to grab another beer.*
>
> *Finally, an hour into my journey, my heroic determination and perseverance pays off as I meet Lgelya (a.k.a. Lara) on YouTube. In a photo slideshow, Lara, who now lives in North Dakota, takes me from Zarafshan's beginning as a mining city that sprung from the desert in the 1960s to more recent times, when the city was considered*

the center of Uzbekistan's gold industry and the home base for the nearby Muruntau open pit mine. Lara lived for 20 years in the city, and the photos show a family building snowmen, working in the mines, and sharing meals. There are camels (!), more turtles (!!) and some smiling people (!!!). Back in the day, there were motorcycle races and swimming races and people selling food. So, if you physically follow in my digital footsteps, it is possible you will find people there. Poor them. Poor you.

He said "Poor them. Poor you" due to his impressions from his virtual travel there. But for us, Zarafshan and the Kyzylkum Desert were part of our lives, a very logical place for us to live and we did not know different. A harsh environment was offset by the special spirit and friendship of people. In a way, it was a gift of life, too.

After we visited China and Hong Kong in 2012, I published "My China Diary" on the Internet, but now I'm thinking of making a book from it, as well as from my travel notes to other countries.

From the period of time from 2000 to present we have traveled to the following countries: Chile, Peru, Ecuador, Panama, Columbia, Switzerland, Italy, Portugal, Spain, France, England, Netherlands, Belgium, Iceland, Norway, Sweden, Denmark, Germany, Poland, Estonia, Finland, Russia, Ukraine, China, Hong Kong, Mexico, Costa Rica, and the Caribbean Islands. Alaska was the most memorable trip inside the United States. I think travel is the only thing that makes one richer for the money spent.

Traveling leaves you speechless, then turns you into a storyteller.

I believe that when you can do things you love, it is a precious gift of life, too. I'm so grateful for all these precious gifts of my life.

Epilogue

From January 2017 to January 2021, I was terrified to watch the onset of Trump's tyranny in our country. I saw such familiar signs—I experienced all of them in the Soviet Union! I ran for a better life from the country where I was born. The Soviet Union controlled its citizens with a regime of tyranny. This regime sustained itself in political power by controlling mass media that was disseminating propaganda, by the secret police, by restrictions of free speech and criticism, by mass surveillance and political purges, by the persecution of specific groups of people. The Constitution in the United States was designed to prevent tyranny through a system of checks and balances. We might be tempted to think that our democratic heritage automatically protects us, but in President Trump's America, those safeguards were failing. Trump held the grandiose belief that only he should rule America. Unchecked by cowed or complicit Republicans in Congress, Trump invoked executive authority to alter policies that were long-established by law and practices. Trump is the only president in the United States who was impeached twice. He came to our lives with a scandal and indecency and he is exiting from our lives with a scandal and indecency.

I'm so relieved that during the election of 2020,

democracy prevailed. But we all witnessed how fragile our democracy is. Even though the horrible Trump presidency is over and Joe Biden won the election of 2020, Trump keeps spreading the lie and pretending that the election was stolen from him.

The January 6, 2021 attack on the U.S. Capitol is one of the most unforgettable events in American history and in my life. The Capitol building was last breached when British forces invaded during the War of 1812. Two hundred and nine years later, a mob of insurrectionists attacked the building at the behest of none other than the sitting, but on-the-way-out, U.S. President Donald Trump. Videos from the scene show Capitol police at worst unprepared and at best overwhelmed by the sheer size of the crowd. I watched on TV in disbelief how easily the rioters were able to enter the Capitol building. Trump supporters invaded the Capitol from multiple points—videos and images show the rioters scaling walls, smashing windows, and breaking down doors to get into and advance through the building. Many lawmakers, including Nancy Pelosi and Mike Pence, were evacuated to safe locations.

Just recently, House Speaker Nancy Pelosi created a select special committee to investigate the attack on the U.S. Capitol on January 6, while most GOP members opposed the creation of the committee.

I'm still worried and wondering what is going to happen during elections in 2022 and 2024 and in what direction this country will be heading?

The year 2020 was one of the hardest years, not only for us personally, but for the entire country, and even the entire world. The COVID-19 pandemic covered the world with darkness and despair. It has led to a dramatic loss of human life worldwide. In the United States, over 600,000 people have died from COVID-19 since January 2020. The coronavirus pandemic was the defining global health crisis of our time and the greatest challenge we have faced since World War II. But the pandemic was much more than a health crisis. It was also an unprecedented socio-economic crisis. Every day, people were losing jobs and income, with no way of knowing when normality would return. Businesses were closing, children were struggling to learn online, and families did not have enough food.

Sparky and I are lucky to be in the stage of our lives when we do not have to worry about our jobs, or income, or how to keep a roof above our heads. We spared ourselves from contracting the virus by being very careful and spending most of the year inside our house. On October 14, 2020, we quietly celebrated our twentieth wedding anniversary during the time of the COVID-19 pandemic.

We got our first Pfizer-BioNTech COVID-19 vaccine as soon as it became available in January-February, 2021. We canceled all our trips that were planned a long time ago. Instead, I spent my time writing this story, a story of our family, a story of my journey from Ukraine to the Kyzylkum Desert, through immigration to freedom, from Buffalo, NY to the shores of sunny Florida in the United States.

***

Life is a long journey. Life is extremely interesting and is a source of joy, but at the same time, it is hard and complicated. Anything can happen in life—unexpected surprises, ups and downs, injustice, betrayal, luck, or tragedy. Life's adversities help people become stronger. As they say, in order to harden steel, a high temperature needs to be created. As a camel from Kyzylkum, I plan to keep going through my life journey, swaying like a ship on the waves of time—the high temperature of life's hardships and troubles makes me stronger. Even among the weeds and thorns of life, one can blossom. The main thing is to never give up on your dreams and to be yourself.

Never regret a day in your life: good days give you happiness, bad days give you experience, the worst days give you lessons, and the best days give you memories.

July 2, 2021, Valencia Lakes, Southwest Florida.

SW Florida.

Lara and Sparky.

Charlie and the Ocean.

About the Author

Born in Ukraine and going to school there, Lara Gelya went on for the next 20 years to the Kyzylkum Desert of the Republic of Uzbekistan, working at geological sites and expeditions of the Mining Industry. At that time Ukraine and Uzbekistan were parts of one country—the Soviet Union.

In 1989 Lara left the Soviet Union, lived in Austria and Italy before she, at last, found her way to the United States in 1990. Starting her life from ground zero again, and trying on so many hats, she was able to make a lengthy professional career that led to her eventual retirement on the shores of sunny Florida. Lara's debut book "Camel from Kyzylkum" is a poignant memoir about hope, struggles, loss, and finding the strength and inspiration to reach again and again for a better life.

When she isn't writing or making her videos and pictures, Lara spends most of her time reading, gardening, cooking, traveling the world, wandering through nature, or catching her favorite shows.

www.ingramcontent.com/pod-product-compliance
Lightning Source LLC
Chambersburg PA
CBHW030906080526
44589CB00010B/173